Spaghetti

To my wife, Barbara

Bodo A. Schieren

Spaghetti

**Special
Editions**

Published in Germany in 1988 by Südwest Verlag GmbH & Co KG, Munich.
Published in the UK in 1993 by Transedition Books,
11-15 The Vineyard, Abingdon, Oxon OX14 3PX, England.

German language edition and photographs © Südwest Verlag GmbH & Co KG, 1988
American language edition © Transedition Books 1993
All rights reserved

Photography: Bodo A Schieren
Recipes and food arrangement: Gisela Lubbe-Zimmermann
Translation: Judith Hayward in association with First Edition Translations Ltd, Cambridge
Reproduction: Colortechnik GmbH, Munich

BDD Special Editions
An Imprint of BDD Promotional Book Company, Inc.
1540 Broadway
New York, N.Y. 10036

BDD Special Editions and the accompanying logo are trademarks of the BDD Promotional Book Company, Inc.

This edition published in the United States of America in 1993 by BDD Special Editions

ISBN 0 7924 5855 9

Printed in 1993 in Slovenia

Contents

All About Noodles

In the thirteenth century, as the story goes, a Venetian merchant traveled to China, spent many years at the court of the Khan and returned to his native land with the 'discovery' of how to make noodles. Although this tale has been repeated widely and for centuries, it is certainly not true. In just one place in his book Marco Polo, the traveler in question, talks about fresh, rather than dried, noodles that he had eaten on his journey, describing how a kind of flour was made from the bark of the sago palm tree. This alone was the remarkable novelty, not the making of noodles themselves, with which he would have been well acquainted.

Scholars who study the history of food believe that pasta developed independently in different areas of the world. When people began to cultivate cereals, they learned to grind the grains between stones to make them more digestible and more versatile. They stirred the flour into water and pressed the resulting dough into flat cakes, which could be cooked on hot stones. In the course of time they found they could roll out the dough into thin sheets, which they then cut into strips and added to soups or stews. Fresh pasta of this type was certainly known both in the Mediterranean area and in China.

Historical finds indicate how popular noodles were even in antiquity. It is claimed that pictures on an Etruscan tomb dating from the fourth century BC and apparently showing a flour bag, a pastry board, dough tongs, a rolling pin, and a small pastry wheel are the earliest evidence of the existence of pasta not just in Italy, but anywhere. And although noodles were known in China in the first century BC, the earliest known recipes using a form of pasta are in a Roman cookbook that may date from the fourth century AD. What happened when the German tribes overran Italy is not known. Eating habits certainly changed – probably for the invaders as well as the invaded – but just as certainly the basic preparatory processes used in Roman cooking were not forgotten. However, as people in the Middle Ages were less concerned with bodily pleasures than with the salvation of their souls, there are no relevant records.

With the dawn of the Renaissance and the deliberate, systematic rediscovery of the antique world, the picture altered. Humankind and its customs came under increasing scrutiny, and people began to take an interest in secular matters. The first descriptions of food began to appear in the thirteenth century. Indications of quality were precisely noted down, and the source of certain products given – Parmesan, for example, from Parmigiano Reggiano. Nutrition was at last being approached not only from a practical but also from a theoretical point of view, and consideration was given to the production and storage of food. People were no longer satisfied with what God gave; they were trying to make themselves independent of the seasons. Finally, in a document from Genoa dated February 4, 1279, we find the term "macaroni" applied for the first time to dried noodles.

The Arabs made a vital contribution to the development of noodles around this time, possibly as early as the eleventh century, although we do not know whether they had the idea themselves or adopted it from the nomadic tribes of the Near East: the drying of fresh noodles. This meant that the noodles could be preserved, thus becoming a constantly available basic foodstuff that could be quickly prepared for caravans crossing the desert and on military campaigns. It was also the Arabs who introduced the art of forming strands of dough with a

hole in the middle – so that the dough could dry out thoroughly and did not become moldy – to Sicily and southern Italy. Pasta-makers quickly learned how to make the dough as thin as possible and roll it around sticks. (Even today many a Neapolitan *mamma* makes her Sunday macaroni in this way; the only difference is that instead of wooden rods she uses metal or plastic knitting needles.) They suspended the noodles over poles so that they hung straight down and placed them in the sun to dry. If rain was forecast, special bells were rung so that the noodle-makers could quickly take their wares under cover.

The Arabs had already realized that the more gluten the flour contains, the thinner the dough could be rolled out, as gluten makes the dough less elastic. A special raw product was required for this purpose, and semolina from durum wheat was imported from Asia Minor and Russia. Eventually, durum wheat was also grown in Italy.

The making of noodles and other forms of pasta soon developed into a skilled craft. The center of production came to be the coast and area around Naples, and the coast of Amalfi. New shapes were constantly being invented and today hardly anyone knows all the names, particularly as the terminology varies in different regions of Italy. Nor is the origin of the name always clear. We know that "macaroni" comes from the Latin word *maccare,* meaning "to press" or "knead".Originally, "macaroni" referred to all kinds of pasta, especially freshly kneaded pasta. However, it soon became established for pasta in the shape of a short tube, while the long solid strands were called *vermicelli,* little worms, although they were, of course, still thicker than our present-day spaghetti, which derives its name from *spago,* meaning string. Today macaroni and spaghetti are used universally, while other terms reflect regional variations. Thus, for example, bucatini, a long noodle with a hollow center, may also be labeled perciatelli; taglierini may be known as fettucine, and spaghettini might also be called linguine. Each of these pastas might be known by other names too, and it is best to look for the shape you want rather than worry about the name.

In a seventeenth-century comedy a Sicilian is contemptuously dismissed by his Neapolitan rival in love as a *mangia-maccheroni,* or macaroni-eater. The Sicilian retaliates by calling the Neapolitan a *sporco mangia-foglie,* a filthy leaf-eater, referring to cabbage soup, which was then a much more popular dish than pasta in Naples. However, the name was soon transferred to the leaves of pasta that the Neapolitans used to prepare their beloved *pasticcios.* Pasta achieved its true destiny with the triumphant appearance of the tomato, first in Neapolitan cooking and then in Italian cooking in general. The first tomatoes taken to Europe from the New World in the sixteenth century were yellow and did not gain widespread acceptance immediately. The red variety was introduced to Italy from America in the mid-eighteenth century and became a basic ingredient in many pasta dishes within a couple of decades.

When Goethe was staying in Naples in 1787–8 he was enthusiastic about the many street stalls where macaroni was cooked, seasoned and sold on a sheet of paper. People ate noodles with their fingers, tilting their heads back and slipping the pasta into their mouths. It may not have been very elegant, but it was entertaining. Eating pasta is not a solemn business today either, but a happy, hearty feast, even if people now use a fork, and possibly a spoon. Some people claim that spaghetti and macaroni contributed to the development of the modern fork: refined people did not like eating with their fingers, so the two- or three-prong meat forks were adapted for the purpose and given four short prongs. We can now conveniently wind the seemingly endless strands of pasta around the prongs and convey them safely to our mouths.

In Pontedassio near Imperia on the Ligurian coast there is a museum devoted to spaghetti. There you can find virtually everything relating to noodles in general and spaghetti in particular: historical documents, written and illustrated history, old processes and manufacturing machines – an entire museum devoted to a fundamentally important foodstuff that gives great pleasure.

With the emergence of powerful hydraulic presses, spaghetti became the number one pasta worldwide. As a *pasta asciutta* (dried pasta), spaghetti forms the ideal basis for simple, cheap, nutritious, quick everyday cooking. For Italians, it is an indispensable component of the menu plan of every domestic and professional cook. If we turn the

ideas of the futuristic writer Emilio Marinetti upside down – he wrote a manifesto glorifying war and condemning dried pasta because it makes people lax and peaceable – we can only hope that the victorious campaign of pasta continues and that it conquers every kitchen in the world by peaceful means.

Homemade Pasta

"Take..." – the literal-minded reader then expects exact figures and precise quantities. But the Italian woman (making pasta is a woman's province) takes a huge bowl, fills it with a frightening quantity of flour, makes a hollow in the center and breaks as many eggs into it as she needs, generally one per person. She adds one or two tablespoons of olive oil and a good pinch of salt. Now she's ready to begin the real work, the kneading. The woman crumbles the mixture into a coarse, dry dough using just her fingers, while allowing the eggs to absorb only as much flour as they actually require. She then lifts the ball of dough from the bowl and kneads it repeatedly on a marble slab – pressing it down with the palm of her hand, drawing it back up and pressing it flat yet again – until it is smooth. She covers the remaining flour in the bowl and sets it aside for the next time.

An Italian woman knows how the dough should be prepared, but has no idea how many ounces of flour the eggs will absorb. This practical knowledge is superior to our dull recipe instructions; types of flour can vary considerably, and not all eggs are the same size. Depending various conditions, flour contains more or less moisture and is more or less glutinous, so for a perfect dough you sometimes need more and sometimes less liquid. And what about the eggs? Three 3-oz. eggs bind as much flour as four 2-oz. eggs!

So try to work along the same principles as an Italian woman, although you can dispense with the big bowl – it is worth having only if you make pasta every day. You can equally well sieve the flour straight onto the marble slab (this is ideal because dough comes away from marble more easily), a pastry board or some other completely smooth, clean work-surface. Make a well, and add salt and eggs. Ideally, the eggs should be of the best quality, with one 2-oz. egg per cup of flour. Next add just a little oil. Add water only if the eggs and oil have not absorbed all the flour, and then add it a drop at a time so that the dough does not go watery in places. Finally, if you do not have a machine (see p. 13) and are having to do everything by hand, add a splash of oil and knead for ten minutes until the dough is smooth, as firm as possible, and definitely not sticky! People who knead pasta every day have enough strength in their fingers and arms to be able to produce a firm dough based on three cups of flour and four eggs without getting tired, sufficient to serve five or six people as a main course. Anyone who embarks on the task only occasionally will soon tire; a pasta machine is then both useful and welcome.

Basic recipe

3½ cups all-purpose flour
4 eggs
good pinch of salt
1–2 tablespoons olive oil and some water, as needed

Knead into a dough as described above. Allow the dough to rest at room temperature for 30 to 60 minutes so that it can be rolled out easily.

Shape the dough into lumps the size of a tennis ball. On a surface lightly dusted with flour roll out each lump with a rolling pin covered in flour, rolling alternately in all directions.

When the dough is paper-thin, cut it into wide or narrow strips – tagliatelle or taglierini. You cannot make spaghetti like this: you wouldn't really want to roll each strip into a noodle!

The flour

Pasta can be made from every kind of flour, but a certain proportion of gluten is essential so that the dough becomes smooth, producing pasta that is nice and firm rather than hard and dry. Gluten consists of proteins that swell when moisture is added to the flour; they begin to work like a glue, giving the dough firmness, stability and elasticity at the same time. The finer the flour, the quicker the gluten is released and swells. Fine durum wheat semolina, which is used commercially to produce the best pasta, has the highest gluten content. At home normal white flour is generally used, as it requires less strength and ensures a good result. Dough made from flour that is rich in gluten must be left to swell or be thoroughly kneaded with strong (machine) pressure.

Gluten in flour that has been more intensively ground or in whole grain flour is less easy to activate, so the dough does not become as pliable. Leaving it to rest does not make much difference. Although it is hard to work with, wholewheat dough still has to be rolled out quite thinly because the gluten draws moisture during cooking, and thick wholewheat noodles become hard when they are boiled.

The pasta machine

The principle of an inexpensive hand-operated pasta machine for home use is as simple as it is effective: the dough is first kneaded between two smooth rollers, then rolled out thinner and thinner, and finally cut into ribbons between two cutting rollers set for wide or narrow strips. There are only a few models that also have a pair of rollers that will shape and divide the dough into strings of spaghetti. So generally these machines are used to prepare tagliatelle or taglierini. Of course, the dough can also be left in sheets for lasagna or cut into whatever shapes are wanted with a knife, wheel or cutter.

Mix the dough roughly and knead it on a floury surface, as described above. The dough becomes smoother and more pliable from passing repeatedly between the rollers. It is best initially to keep the piece of dough too thick rather than too thin, for the more often it is squeezed through the rollers, the better and more thoroughly the flour and the moisture mix, and the better the gluten is released. The forces at work here are considerably greater than when the kneading is done by hand, so it is not necessary for this dough to be left to rest before it is rolled out.

Next, dust the dough with flour and press it through the rollers fixed at their widest setting. The dough must be dry enough not to stick to the rollers. (If this happens the first time you push the dough through, abandon the machine – cleaning, washing, and drying the rollers takes ages – and continue by hand.) Dust lightly with flour again, shape into a square, and pass between the rollers again. Repeat this process at least six times – or better still, ten times – turning the dough 90 degrees each time you pass it between the rollers so that it is thoroughly kneaded in every direction. The dough is ready when the surface has a nice sheen. The sheet of dough should end up the same width as the rollers. Now reduce the gap between the rollers by one or two notches (depending on the model) each time you pass the dough between them. This makes the shape of the dough consistently longer and thinner. Handle the dough carefully, and after each rolling dust it very lightly with flour, or rub a light coating of flour into it, so that the lengths of pasta do not stick together if they touch or are decoratively laid over one another in folds to save space.

Important Utensils

Wooden fork or
spoon

Large pot

Garlic press

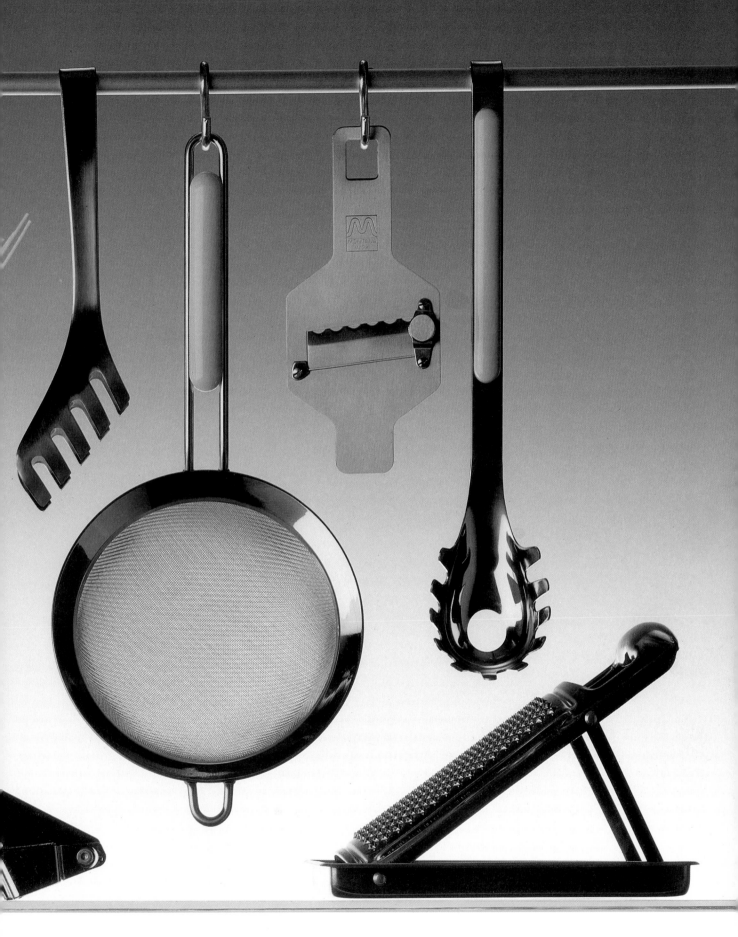

Serving tongs   Strainer   Mushroom slicer   Spaghetti ladle   Cheese grater

15

Cooking Pasta Is Easy...

Anyone who thinks that all you have to do is to throw some pasta into water and boil it until it is soft is, of course, mightily mistaken. Let there be no doubt: pasta is demanding and needs personal, careful, perfect treatment.

The first consideration – after choosing top-quality pasta – is getting the timing right. Pasta does not wait for the eater; the guest must be ready and waiting for the pasta. The bad habit practiced by many a cook of preparing pasta in advance and warming it up at the crucial moment is not just reprehensible; in the case of spaghetti it is inexcusable: only freshly cooked spaghetti tastes just right, is *al dente* (see p. 20 for details), and interacts correctly with the sauce (see also pp. 22-5).

The principle for cooking spaghetti properly is very simple: as there is not much to watch out for, pay attention to even the minutest details. Attach great importance to secondary considerations, and look for the hidden significance in apparently logical actions. Do not let all this confuse you – even experts are not entirely unanimous about every theory or every thing that can or might play a role. There is always more than one way of doing things, and there is a whole host of useful hints and tricks.

Some people, for example, add a dash of olive oil to the cooking water, others a piece of butter. This is intended to prevent the pasta from sticking together. However, if you move the pasta around from time to time with a fork, this will not happen in any case. Besides, the action of the water briskly boiling ensures that the pasta is constantly moving. Of course, oil and butter further prevent sticking, but they also have another effect, which may have negative consequences: the surface of the pasta gets covered with a light film of grease and therefore is less receptive to the sauce. The sauce may simply "fall" through the spaghetti.

There is also a heated debate about rinsing the pasta after it is boiled. Should it simply be turned into a colander and quickly drained, or should it be rinsed under cold running water? A cold rinse certainly stops the cooking process in its tracks and washes off any starch on the surface of the pasta. Admittedly, the pasta does not stick, but later the sauce can hardly combine with it either – the sauce has to be very thick with a good consistency and not too greasy, otherwise it slips off the pasta. Nonetheless, many Italian women succeed admirably, while pasta experts tend not to rinse. See pp. 18-19 for all that has to be borne in mind.

There is complete unanimity on at least one point: to start, you need a large pot and lots of water!

Step by step: the golden rules for cooking pasta to perfection

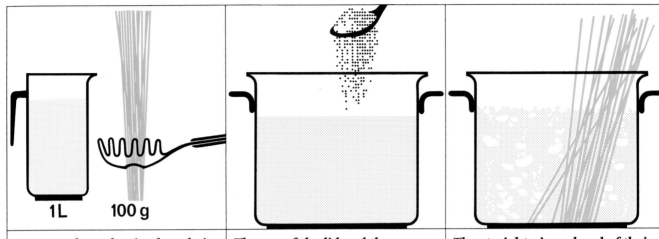

Water and spaghetti – the relative quantities exactly defined

The rule of thumb is child's play: for every 3 oz. of pasta bring 4 cups of water to the boil. However, not many people know what lies behind the rule and why it is so important to observe it. Pasta is always put into briskly boiling water, and it must be kept on the boil throughout the cooking. If it is placed in a relatively small quantity of water, the water immediately cools down and stops boiling, and the pasta gets tough and sticky. If there is enough water, however, it does not stop boiling. Thus, in Italian restaurants there is always a gigantic pot of boiling water on the stove, often holding as much as 10 gallons.

What about cooking pasta at home? Well, it is best always to add 4 to 8 cups of water to the basic quantity. Thus, if you are cooking 3 to 4 oz. of spaghetti per person as a main dish for a family of four, you should use at least 16 or, even better, 24 cups of water. While you are waiting for the water to boil you have time to measure the amount of spaghetti you need.

The use of the lid and the function of salt

How quickly the water comes to the boil depends on a lot of things, particularly the efficiency of the stove and the amount of heat provided. But there are two other factors of equal importance. First, the better the bottom of the pot fits on the source of heat, the less energy will be wasted. Therefore, the pot should be slightly larger than the ring, never smaller. If you have an electric stove, it is even more important that the bottom of the pot, when it is hot, should sit quite flat on the cooking surface.

The second point applies to all types of energy and pots: when bringing the water to the boil, put the lid on the pot. Not only do you considerably shorten the time needed, but also you use only about half as much energy.

Do not add salt until the water is boiling; then use 1 heaping teaspoon. It sounds a lot, but hardly any of the salt is eaten. It does, however, improve the taste and consistency of the pasta.

The straight pieces bend of their own accord

When the salt is added, the boiling water bubbles up with an added surge of heat. To exploit this, put the spaghetti straight into the pot. Do not put the spaghetti into the water in a tight bundle – fan it out loosely so that the pieces do not stick together.

Even if you have used a large pot, you will note that the spaghetti will not fit – the ends of these long pieces stick out. There was a time when worthy cooks broke the spaghetti so that it would all disappear into the pot, even a small pot, immediately. But don't do it – we are not adding pasta to soup! Before long the spaghetti will soften, and begin to bend and curl up in the pan. You can give a helping hand when the parts already submerged become pliable, but, in any case, you do not have to wait long for the spaghetti to slip into the water of its own accord.

Keep free by stirring

When all the spaghetti is submerged, and as the water continues to boil briskly on maximum heat, it is a good idea to loosen it by stirring. Traditionally, a wooden fork or spoon is used for this. Metal is not used, perhaps because wood has rounded edges with no sharp corners that might damage or cut the pasta, or perhaps because it does not conduct the heat of the boiling water to your hand. You do not need to stir for long, but initially you can loosen potential tangles or clumps of strands that are beginning to coagulate. All the strands should be floating free.

The water must boil hard the whole time, which means that the lid cannot be used. It is true that this wastes a lot of energy, but if you leave pasta simmering gently in a covered pan, it becomes tough and slimy. And if you cover the pan when the water is boiling hard, the protein escapes from the pasta and the pot boils over.

How spaghetti gets its "bite"

The magic formula in Italian is *al dente* – "for the tooth"! This means having something to bite on. It is not always easy to decide when that point has been reached. As well as experience, it requires constant checking, as all sorts of pasta are different. As pasta boils, the flour in it absorbs moisture from the cooking water, it swells and the pasta softens. Thus the longer pasta is in water, the more "watery" it will become. So it is a question of discovering the point at which the center of a noodle, for example, has been able to absorb sufficient water to lose its dry hardness and can be bitten into easily. When this point is reached, the outer layers should not yet be slimy or beginning to disintegrate. Obviously, the time it takes for this to happen will vary depending on the thickness of the pasta. The only way to be certain is to check the stage the pasta has reached by tasting it towards the end of probable cooking time – two to five minutes in the case of fresh spaghetti, and at least twice as long for dried.

Draining

When you have established that the spaghetti is *al dente*, or ready, tasting at its best, you must remove it from its cooking water without delay. In restaurants where constantly boiling water is needed for pasta, the cooked pasta is lifted out of its bubbling cauldron with a colander. Many chefs, hard though it is to believe, use their bare hands – habit seems to have desensitized them. However, they do immediately place their hands under cold running water, knowing that the cold will immediately counteract the effects of the heat (the whole business is over so quickly that you have to watch like a hawk to see what is going on). This dangerous practice – and imitation is certainly not recommended – clearly shows that you can rinse freshly cooked pasta with cold water, abruptly stopping any further cooking. But while the shock is no doubt beneficial for the hands, it may not be so good for the pasta, as explained on p. 17; you are safer just to drain the pasta quickly. That sounds quite simple, but needs to be expanded, so see p. 22.

Perfect Al Dente

or the difficult art of cooking spaghetti just right: pasta you can bite on!

Anyone who buys spaghetti can take the easy way out and claim that the package tells you how long it takes to cook. This information is always valuable as an approximate guide, as well as being an indication of quality. As a rule, top-quality pasta is made only from durum wheat semolina, and this requires longer cooking than the sort made from durum wheat flour, or even ordinary soft wheat flour of the type used for baking.

If you have made the pasta yourself, it is much more difficult to say how long it will take to cook. On the one hand it depends what flour you have used, and on the other how dry the pasta is. The more gritty the flour and the drier the pasta, the longer it will take to cook.

Neither experienced domestic cooks nor professional pasta chefs can predict simply by looking at the pasta exactly when it is cooked to the proverbial perfection; that is, when it is smooth on the outside and in the center has a barely perceptible speck that is still lighter in color but no longer white. At that moment the spaghetti is not yet soft, not boiled to extinction; instead it has an alluring, almost living tension.

You can see this if you lift out a strand to test it. It should fall over the fork in an arc, but ought not to hang completely limp. But let's not rely on our eyes alone, let's test more closely in the classic, time-honored way by biting into it, simply biting off the end of some spaghetti. The outside should not stick to your teeth, and inside there should be the speck described above. Especially in the case of spaghetti made from durum wheat semolina that has been kept for some time, the test may have to be repeated several times before the crucial point of readiness is reached. As you see, pasta cannot be cooked by the clock! When you have finally got that far, you must pour away the water immediately, for pasta stays at the point of perfection for just a few seconds.

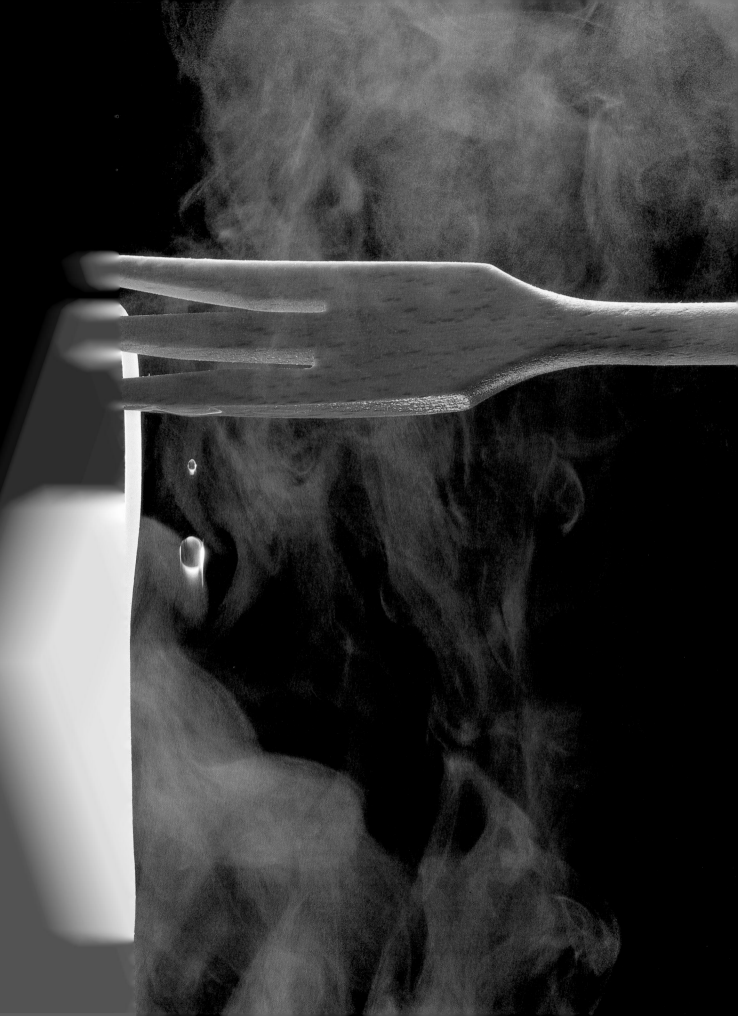

Draining

When the spaghetti has reached its ideal condition in briskly boiling salted water, tip it into a sieve or colander. The water runs off, but initially the spaghetti is still moist. While it is in this state place the spaghetti in a bowl, preferably preheated, and immediately combine it with its sauce or butter, oil, or cheese. Do not rinse the pasta under cold water unless you are preparing a spaghetti salad. The whole process, from draining to serving, should take only a few seconds. If at any point your speed slackens or your concentration fails, the resulting damage will be difficult to repair.

If you leave the pasta in the colander for even just a minute, some of the moisture caught up in it evaporates, the surface sets and can no longer absorb the sauce – the pasta slips around in it. You can remedy this to some extent by sprinkling a dash of the water drained from the pasta over it, but be careful – the pasta must not be covered with water again.

If, on the other hand, you do not allow a little time for the cooking water to drain away, the pasta will be too wet and will dilute the sauce. You have to bear in mind that different sauces adhere to the pasta more or less well – a creamy sauce, for example, adheres better than a clear one; one bound with egg yolk better than one based on butter. A very thick sauce tends to require moister pasta; a very liquid one, dryish pasta.

At the same time you must remember that even now the hot spaghetti may start to stick together. So shake the colander around while the pasta is draining, which will also prevent it from drying out on top – the spaghetti will remain perfect!

Combining pasta with sauce

Once the drained spaghetti has landed safely in the preheated bowl, it eagerly awaits further attention: it must at once be turned over with a generous piece of butter or mixed with its sauce, whether this is a gravy or more of a stew, so that it does not dry out and so that the still-moist surface can immediately combine sublimely with the sauce.

If the pasta is not turned over at once and carefully, it dries out and forms those hard crusts that have so often ruined people's gastronomic pleasure. If you are determined to serve the pasta and the sauce separately so that the guests can help themselves, a little butter at least or, depending on your taste and the sauce to go with it, possibly olive oil is necessary to keep the pasta soft and smooth. Butter is safest: the outer surface of the pasta, with its coating of starch, combines particularly well with very cold butter cut up into small pieces and mixed into it. If the spaghetti is really hot, the same process occurs as when you make a butter sauce: the melting butter combines perfectly with the moisture and does not form an oily lake in the middle of the pasta.

Never add all the sauce to the pasta if it is to be served as a main course. It is better to keep back at least half of it so that everyone can help themselves to as much as they want.

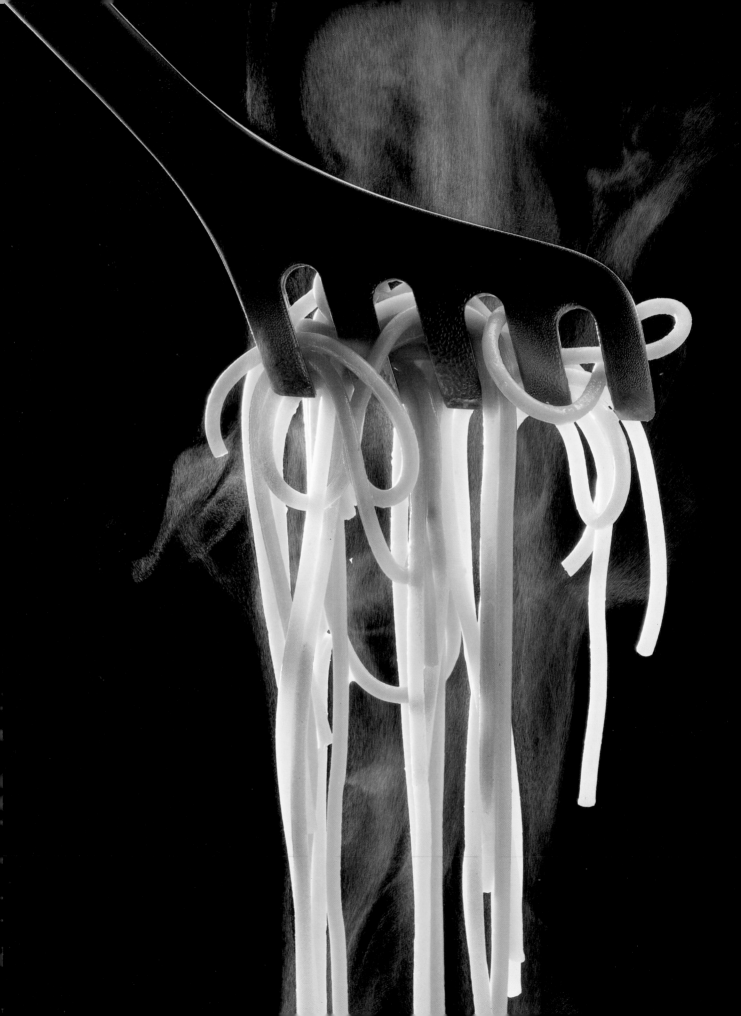

Serving Spaghetti

There was a time when a large bowl of steaming pasta was placed on the family table, and everyone reached out to eat from the communal dish. With increasing prosperity each person was given an individual plate and nowadays the Italian *mamma* gives everyone an appropriate helping, large or small. She does it skillfully; like a chef or a waiter, she has gained practice in dealing with awkward things. And some types of pasta, spaghetti in particular, have a knack of either escaping just as you have carefully got hold of them, linking together in a far longer chain than anticipated, or getting tangled up in unmanageable portions. If you look round a table of averagely experienced spaghetti eaters, you will always find some reason to feel lighthearted at their efforts. A meal involving spaghetti can never be a solemn affair.

A great many implements have been dreamt up to divide spaghetti into suitable portions with decorum and get it out of the bowl and safely onto the plate without ruining the tablecloth. There are lifters and tongs made of metal or wood. Of course you can learn how to use them, but given a modicum of dexterity you can manage just as well with an ordinary fork and spoon – it is just a matter of eating spaghetti often enough. It has now become common practice to do what has always been customary in restaurants: to serve individual portions on a dinner plate or a soup plate. That way, the chef can deal with the fair sharing out of the pasta in the kitchen without any smug comments, and wipe off any sauce spilt on the edge of a plate with a piece of paper towel. And the skill of your guests is not tested until it comes to the eating.

A cheese grater can be put on the table so that everyone can grate a portion of cheese onto the pasta. You can also grate the cheese with a vegetable grater or with a food processor (if you do this, take care that the cheese does not get warm, as this affects its flavor).

The Art of Eating Spaghetti

When spaghetti was "discovered", table manners were still extremely rudimentary and people used to eat pasta only with their hands. As can be seen from old paintings, a portion of spaghetti was taken between the thumb and the index and middle fingers, then raised up as high as was necessary. The head was tipped back and the pasta was allowed to slip into the mouth. No one can deny that this is a very practical way of enjoying spaghetti. At the time the only generally available item of cutlery was the spoon, which was unsuitable for spaghetti. However, from the two-pronged tool used for spearing meat, the fork evolved as a universal implement. Thus the fork came to be used for eating anything that was not too liquid. Its range of uses was extended by giving it first three, then four prongs, which made it easier to manage and meant that it was also suitable for picking up spaghetti. The fork was simply rotated in the mass of spaghetti in order to gather some up, with or without the help of a spoon. Now there are even special spaghetti forks that make it quicker and easier to pick up pasta. These are fun as a gimmick, for children, or as a small gift for the pasta fan who has everything.

Some people take a knife, hack the spaghetti into short pieces and eat it with a spoon, but this is just not acceptable: knives are out of place in a pasta dish.

1

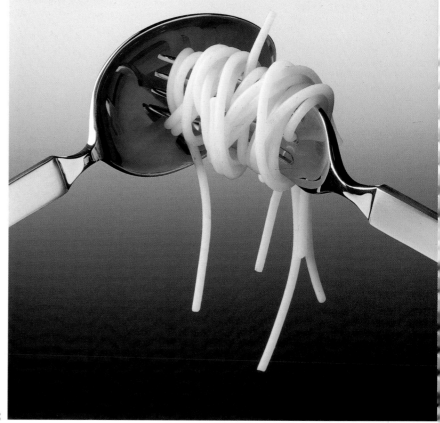

2

1

Here is one way it can be done: pick up a few strands of spaghetti on your fork and convey them to your mouth. But there is a problem – you have to suck hard to get them all in. Spaghetti hanging from your mouth does not look very pretty, you have to lean over the plate in a rather inelegant manner, and your lips get totally covered in sauce. So follow the first step and pick up a few strands of spaghetti on your fork – just do not eat them yet!

2

The helpful custom of using the spoon as a base on which to rotate the fork became widespread in Italy when the whole family used to eat from the same bowl. It is no less practical today, for even those who have not had very much practice can eat easily and elegantly with this method.

3

Place the fork on the plate with the prongs at right angles to the surface. Now turn the fork until all the strands of spaghetti are wound around the prongs. If you use the sloping edge of the plate, you no longer have to hold the fork upright and can achieve a very well-mannered effect by inclining it.

4

This is how the perfectly wound mouthful of spaghetti should look: no strands are hanging down, and the fork can be placed in the mouth without touching the lips, so no slurping! Buon appetito.

Recipes with Vegetables and Herbs

Dictionary of Ingredients

Artichokes Because of their bitterness, which stimulates the appetite, globe artichokes go very well with pasta. Small, young artichokes with purple tips are best: their hearts can be used whole. Only the base of larger artichokes can be used with pasta, the leaves and the choke being completely discarded.

Asparagus There are two types of this delicious sprouting vegetable. Completely white asparagus is usually grown on raised beds, earthed up and harvested before it pierces the ground. The tops of green asparagus are purple or green, as it is picked when the tip or the whole spear has emerged above the ground (chlorophyll builds up as a result of exposure to the light). Green asparagus has a more "vegetably" taste, a bit like peas. Wild asparagus is thinner and has a stronger flavor.

Avocados These fruits – the full name is "avocado pear" – have a high fat content and have been described as "butter from the forest". Be careful which kind you buy. The thick-skinned, purple-brown Hass variety have the best flavor; the next best are the large Nabal variety and the soft-skinned Fuerte and Ettinger types, on which dark patches on the skin indicate overripeness. Always buy avocados a few days before you want to use them and let them ripen at home at room temperature.

Basil A herb so indispensable that Italian cooking is inconceivable without it, as its aromas combine ideally with tomato. There are different varieties of basil, with fine, oregano-type, salad, or purple leaves. The small-leaf variety is good only in sauces, preferably added at the beginning of cooking; raw it has a pungent, almost bitter taste. Oregano-type leaves can be used for all purposes, adding a pleasant aroma either gently cooked or raw. The large-leaf salad variety is best eaten raw. The rare purple type can be used for everything and it also looks very attractive.

Broccoli Both the buds and the stems of this brassica are eaten. Buy only young, tight, very green heads, and blanch the buds and refresh them under cold water to retain the green color.

Carrots There are two types of carrot: stump-rooted and long, tapering. All carrots should be eaten young and sweet. As they get older the bright orange outer ring tastes considerably nicer than the paler center.

Celery Sticks of celery should be fresh and crisp, and any strings running down the back should be removed.

Cheese Parmesan, which is regarded as the "king of cheeses" has been served with pasta for centuries. Regulations governing the making of Parmigiano Reggiano, to give it its proper name, were first laid down in the thirteenth century, the very time from which the first definite records of Italian pasta date. Was this a remarkable coincidence or the first sign of the coming Renaissance? Whatever the answer, cheese and pasta became inseparable. A spoonful of grated Parmesan strewn over the steaming spaghetti mixed with sauce. . .what harmony there is in this culinary marriage!

The fundamental condition for enthusiasm on this topic is, of course, perfect Parmesan. Amazingly, the name is not protected – any dry grated cheese can be called Parmesan, even if it has been put together from a grated mixture of old, dried-up leftover cheese that was actually defective when it was fresh. For this reason, never buy it already grated; always buy a piece of true old Parmesan, Parmigiano Reggiano stravecchio. You cannot mistake it because the name is written into the rind. It is not cheap, but it is the best on the market. Wrapped in plastic wrap or wax paper, it will keep quite well in the vegetable compartment of a refrigerator for a few weeks; if you take it out and leave it at room temperature for two hours before using it, it will lose none of its flavor.

Choose carefully and pay special attention to the age of the cheese, which is all-important for the taste: the basic rule is that the milder the sauce, the less mature the cheese should be.

Many dishes require very young, fresh cheeses that are meant to melt in the sauce or over the pasta. Then what is needed is top-quality fontina, Gorgonzola or mozzarella. Even medium-quality cheese that tastes fine on a piece of bread will impart a coarse, intrusive quality to a sauce, and not give it the required subtlety. All cheeses reveal their true character to a discerning palate when they have been heated, and the saying "A dish can never taste better than its poorest ingredient" was never more applicable.

Cream Mild creamy sauces are the epitome of the lavish cooking of the Po plain and the fertile valleys of northern Italy. Cream and butter are used generously to produce the rich sauces that coat and enhance the pasta.

Use fresh (not heat-treated) light or heavy cream. Crème fraîche is used less often, as its sharper flavor does not always blend with the pasta.

Eggplants These round or club-shaped vegetables range in color from purple to almost black. They ought to be sun-ripened, not grown in greenhouses. The skin should be tight, and the stem green. Do not cut them up until you are about to use them (oxidation alters the flavor), then sprinkle them with salt so that some of the moisture is drawn out.

Fennel This aromatic bulb is tenderest when it is grown in mild climates. Do not buy any with dark blemishes or shriveled outer sheaths.

Garlic Garlic leaves no one indifferent: it divides people into two camps, one adoring it, the other hating it. There is no middle ground either concerning its special aroma: on the one hand it increases the libido, but on the other hand it can have a very offputting effect on a potential partner!

When cooking pasta, garlic is an indispensable ingredient. Not only does garlic have a pleasanter smell when it is young, but the smell is less persistent, the garlic is more digestible and has a milder taste. The cloves should be firm and juicy, not yellow and spongy. If a green shoot has already formed, the clove is too old; you should at least remove the green shoot and blanch the clove.

While young bulbs with skin that is still soft and not papery taste best, they may be relatively expensive and hard to find. Look for medium-sized bulbs with almond-sized cloves; the outside skin should have a purple or brownish sheen. Store garlic in a cool, dry, dark, airy place.

Do not use garlic powder or garlic paste, which always has an unpleasantly old taste.

Garlic burns more quickly than onion, so never put it in at the same time; always add it later. Many Italians add finely diced or flaked garlic just before a dish is ready because the aroma is then at its most subtle. It is also more easily tolerated if it has been cooked for a relatively short time.

If you crush garlic in a press, never leave it standing or it will develop a sulfurous flavor, and never roast or fry it, because it will immediately turn bitter. Always add it to a liquid.

Garlic tastes best in sauces or oil if you crush it to a paste with salt in a mortar. Then just stir it in and serve immediately.

Herbs A wave of enthusiasm for fresh herbs has swept through our kitchens and many a cooking enthusiast prides him- or herself on liberally seasoned sauces where a bit of everything available is popped in to create a glorious muddle. People from the Mediterranean area handle herbs differently, although they are just as liberal with them. An uninterrupted, carefully cultivated tradition means that leaves, flowers, needles or seeds are not used at random, but always to create a definite effect. So it is accepted as a matter of course that one sauce will be seasoned only with a certain herb, while another dish owes its unmistakable character to a particular leaf. There are no flights of fancy, no mixing and muddling. Nor is there the strange belief that seasoning is right only if you do not notice it; quite the reverse: why bother using a herb if you cannot taste it? Pasta, which does not in itself have a strong flavor, is really crying out for powerful accents. And nature has wisely ordained that herbs make pasta easier to enjoy – it is more digestible, and they provide the missing minerals and vitamins.

Dishes tastily prepared with herbs are quite simply better for you than insipid food.

Leeks The white part of the stem has the most delicate flavor. Leeks should be washed very thoroughly and the green leaves should be briefly blanched.

Lemons Good lemons should be a true yellow and not too small. Hard, greenish ones are very acidic and have very little flavor.

Limes This green relation of the lemon has a more intense flavor and is particularly good with fish and seafood.

Mint Of the many varieties, the best known is peppermint, which is pleasant as a medicine, in chewing gum and as a tea. In Italy a milder, more aromatic mint with tenderer leaves is preferred for culinary purposes, and it is also available dried. It must be added with care, as it can impart rather too much of its own flavor to a dish.

Olive oil The best olive oil is *Olio si oliva extra vergine* (extra virgin olive oil), the pure juice of the fruit with no water in it. Legally, the acid content may not exceed 1 percent. Top-quality oils from the best oil-producing areas – Venetia, Liguria, Tuscany, Provence and Catalonia – contain no more than 0.5 percent acid. Oil of this quality can be obtained only if the olives are picked by hand before they are too ripe and pressed without excessive pressure in the cool winter temperature with no added heat. Obviously such oil is not going to be cheap.

It is important to look for the two words *extra vergine. Sopraffino vergine* (up to 1.5 percent acid), *fino vergine* (up to 2 percent) or just *vergine* (up to 3.3 percent) might

lead you to expect something equivalent, but you would be disappointed. Though even simple *vergine* is cold-pressed, the temperature of the press can legally be raised to 113˚F; as neither the pressure nor the quality of the olives is regulated, a lot more can be extracted if the manufacturer goes to the limits of the rules. If at the same time the last dregs of oil in the pressed pulp are released using permitted chemicals, a few more pints can be obtained. This adulteration has an adverse impact on the pocket, taste buds and health of the consumer.

Pure olive oil, another fine-sounding description, is a blend of cold-pressed oil and refined oil; that is, oil extracted from the olives by chemical means and then purified. Finally, there is a mixture of oil extracted from the remaining olive pulp and olive oil, known as *olio de sansa di oliva*.

Extra virgin olive oil can really be compared to wine: the place of origin, the variety of olive, the soil, climate and vintage, and the care with which the olives are harvested and the oil produced leave their mark, and a connoisseur will recognize it. Olive oil should always be stored in a cool, dark place. If it gets too cold, small globules of fat form, which disappear again at room temperature. Never keep olive oil in a refrigerator.

Good olive oil is good for the health. The high level of monounsaturated fatty acids is beneficial in maintaining low blood cholesterol and therefore helping to prevent heart disease and circulatory problems. It helps keep the skin smooth and stimulates the brain. Whenever possible, add a dash of olive oil to a dish at the end of cooking, not only because of what is contains but for flavor.

Olives These are the fruits of the olive tree, and they vary greatly in flavor depending on where they come from, how ripe they are, and how they have been preserved. There are the mild, nutty, green olives, which may be stuffed with peppers, almonds, onions or anchovies; pale purple olives, harvested when half ripe; and the truly black ones with a strong aromatic flavor, which are picked in winter when they are fully ripe. Olives can be plump and juicy or shriveled with an almost prune-like texture. Black olives are often preserved with spices, but naturally flavored ones preserved just in oil are best for cooking.

Onions Of the many different kinds, the mild white or almost sweet purple bulbs are to be preferred if you are using large quantities. The common yellow onion is also fine as a basis for cooking, gently stewed or fried.

Parsley Parsley really needs no introduction. However, the varieties used for cooking in Italy are almost always flat-leaf Italian parsleys, some of which have a distinct aroma of celery.

Peas The most delicious vegetable also gives the most work, which is why canned and frozen peas are so popular. However, fresh peas – if you can get them – taste far better, and peas from your own garden cannot be beaten.

Peppers Sweet peppers change in color from green to yellow or red as they ripen, becoming sweeter in the process. The best for cooking are the fleshy varieties, while thin-skinned ones are better for salads or as a seasoning.

Savoy cabbage This is the finest of the various types of cabbage. Use only the pale green and yellow leaves, and always blanch so that the pungent flavor is reduced and the color fixed.

Scallions Some of these small onions have a round bulb and others are long and leek-like. They are particularly mild and discreet in flavor. The white part can be cooked, but the green part should only be used raw or heated briefly (otherwise it goes slimy).

Shallots Smaller, more delicate relations of the onion. The nicest are the purple or gray round ones, then the purply – brown longish varieties. The yellowy-brown ones are too hard and too hot. Be careful when frying: they produce less moisture than onions and tend to burn.

Snow peas A special sort of pea with pods that have no cellophane-like inner membrane. The pods are harvested before the peas have formed in them.

Spinach Spring spinach is tenderest, dark green winter spinach has most flavor, and light green forced spinach is the most boring.

Tomatoes It is impossible to imagine Italian cooking without tomatoes, yet this American fruit started its triumphal progress in Naples just two hundred years ago. Pasta and tomatoes go together in a number of ways, with the choice of the type of tomato or tomato-based product depending on the dish.

The flesh of raw tomatoes combined with garlic, salt, pepper, and oil and served with hot spaghetti makes a simple, deliciously summery meal. For this you need fleshy beefsteak tomatoes, almost ripe but lightly dappled with green on the outside to add to the freshness. This variety of tomato ripens from inside, with the flesh turning red before the skin. As a salad variety they do not contain any poisonous solanine (the poison typical of nightshade or solanaceous plants), which might be retained in the green parts in other varieties.

Sauces can be made from fresh or canned tomatoes. Fresh tomatoes need only to be crushed, then cooked slowly and thoroughly along with their seeds and skins, and whatever seasoning and other vegetables are required. They should then be strained through a sieve and reduced if necessary.

Plum tomatoes are ideal for sauces, and are readily available peeled and canned.

Tomato purée is made simply from reduced, sieved fruit.

Tomato paste is concentrated tomato purée, single or double strength. It is an ideal base for sauces in which tomato is used as a seasoning and for color, but not much moisture is required. Sun-dried tomatoes should be used only as a seasoning or as a garnish for an appetizer.

Truffles There are black truffles and white truffles, and they are used in completely different ways.

Black truffles, whether fresh or canned, can be used in sauces stewed gently with other vegetables or as a flavoring. White truffles, on the other hand, are best chopped raw over a dish at the last minute when they release their full aroma. They are also available preserved, but are only a pale shadow of their fresh selves.

Watercress The dark green leaves have a sharp refreshing taste – they should be used raw or very quickly blanched.

Zucchini If they are harvested while still small, zucchini taste of hazelnuts. They are rarely sold with their flowers, which can be eaten stuffed, in fritters, or braised.

Spaghetti with garlic, olive oil and chilies

1 lb. spaghetti

salted water

½ cup olive oil

6-8 cloves garlic, finely chopped

½ teaspoon salt

1 small chili pepper, diced

small bunch flat-leaf parsley, chopped

freshly ground pepper

Cook the spaghetti in plenty of salted water until *al dente.*

Meanwhile heat the olive oil in a skillet.

Fry the garlic lightly until it turns golden, then salt.

Add the diced chili pepper and fry gently for a short time.

Mix in the parsley.

Drain the spaghetti.

Mix the spaghetti in a bowl with the olive oil, and sprinkle with freshly ground pepper.

Variations

Use fresh oregano instead of parsley and pass round a bowl of freshly grated Parmesan cheese.

Sprinkle grated pecorino cheese over the dish.

Serves 4
Preparation time: 20 minutes
Calories per portion: 672
Recommended wine: Category 2•1•3

Spaghetti with artichokes

8 small young artichokes

juice of 1 lemon

½ cup olive oil

1 onion, finely chopped

4 cloves garlic, finely chopped

½ glass dry white wine

2 tablespoons chopped mint

salt

freshly ground pepper

2¼ cups light cream

1 lb. spaghetti

salted water

2 tablespoons butter

1 cup freshly grated Parmesan cheese

Break the stems off the artichokes, and discard any hard outer leaves and the tips of the leaves.

Cut the heart and the remaining leaves lengthwise into thin slices and immediately place in lemon juice.

Heat the olive oil in a skillet, and gently fry the chopped onion and garlic in it.

Add the wet artichokes and pour the wine over them.

Cover and cook on a low heat for 15 minutes.

Add 1 tablespoon mint and the cream, and cook for a further 5 minutes, then season with salt and pepper.

Meanwhile cook the spaghetti in plenty of salted water until *al dente*, then drain.

Tip the spaghetti into a preheated bowl, mix in the butter, then add the artichokes and sauce, and sprinkle with the remaining mint.

Sprinkle some of the Parmesan cheese on the pasta, and pass around the rest in a bowl.

Serves 4
Preparation time: 60 minutes
Calories per portion: 1191.7
Recommended wine: Category **1**•**3**•**2**

Spinach taglierini with avocado cream

14 oz. spinach taglierini

salted water

2 large or 3 small ripe avocados

1¾ cups light cream

½ cup grated Parmesan cheese

salt

freshly ground pepper

½ cup ricotta cheese

Cook the spinach taglierini in plenty of salted water until *al dente*, then drain.

Peel the avocados and purée three-quarters of the flesh with the cream.

Mix in the Parmesan cheese.

Season with salt and pepper to taste.

Dice the remaining avocado.

Mix the avocado cream with the pasta.

Serve sprinkled with the diced avocado and ricotta cheese.

Serves 4
Preparation time: 20 minutes
Calories per portion: 1048
Recommended wine: Category **1**•3•2

Spaghetti with tomato sauce

⅜ cup olive oil
1 onion, peeled and finely chopped
3 cloves garlic, finely chopped
3½ lb. ripe tomatoes or canned tomatoes, peeled, deseeded and roughly chopped
1 tablespoon each freshly chopped basil and flat-leaf parsley
salt
freshly ground pepper
1 lb. spaghetti or spaghettini
salted water
½ cup each freshly grated pecorino cheese and Parmesan cheese

Heat the oil, and gently fry the onion and garlic in it until they are transparent.

Add the tomatoes and herbs.

Season with salt and pepper.

Simmer the sauce gently on a low heat for 25 minutes (about 10 minutes longer if using canned tomatoes to allow the juice to evaporate).

Cook the pasta in briskly boiling salted water until *al dente*.

Drain.

Arrange the spaghetti with the tomato sauce and some of the cheese.

Serve the rest of the cheese separately.

Serves 4
Preparation time: 45 minutes
Calories per portion: 782.5
Recommended wine: Category 1 • 3 • 2

Spaghetti with olive sauce

2¼ cups fresh black olives or 1 jar olive paste (obtainable from good Italian shops)

1 onion, finely chopped

½ cup olive oil

1 small bay leaf, crushed

½ teaspoon dried oregano or freshly chopped herbs

5 canned peeled tomatoes, puréed

salt

freshly ground pepper

1 pinch ground cinnamon

14 oz. spaghetti

salted water

12 black olives

Pit the olives, chop them finely and reduce them to a paste with a pestle and mortar.

Lightly brown the chopped onion in 4 tablespoons hot olive oil.

Add the olives, herbs and puréed tomatoes and cook for 5 minutes at a low temperature, stirring constantly.

Add salt, pepper, and cinnamon to taste.

Cook the pasta in plenty of salted water until *al dente*.

Drain.

Mix with the olive paste and the remainder of the olive oil.

Serve garnished with olives.

Serves 4
Preparation time: 60–70 minutes
Calories per portion: 893
Recommended wine: Category 4•3•2

Spaghetti with green asparagus and ham

1 lb. tender green asparagus
¼ cup olive oil
3 tablespoons butter
1 onion, peeled and finely chopped
2 cloves garlic, peeled and finely chopped
1 teaspoon lemon juice
salt
freshly ground pepper
1 bunch basil (wash and pick off the leaves)
14 oz. spaghetti
salted water
6 slices prosciutto, cut into strips ¼ in. wide and 1½ in. long

Discard any tough parts of the stalks, cut the asparagus diagonally into pieces about 1¼ in. long and rinse in cold water.

Heat the oil and butter in a deep skillet, and cook the onions and garlic gently until they are transparent.

Add the asparagus, cook gently, turning, then cover and cook for 5–8 minutes until soft.

Season with lemon juice, salt and pepper to taste.

Mix in the basil.

While the asparagus is cooking boil the spaghetti in plenty of salted water until *al dente*.

Drain.

Mix the pasta with the asparagus and the strips of prosciutto, then serve.

Serves 4
Preparation time: about 30 minutes
Calories per portion: 661
*Recommended wine: Category **2**•1•3*

Spaghetti with lemon sauce

1 lb. spaghetti

salted water

2 tablespoons butter

2 scallions, washed and cut into fine rounds

zest of 1 lemon, pared off in fine strips

¼ cup dry sherry

1½ cups crème fraîche

juice of 1 lemon

salt

freshly ground pepper

small bunch each finely chopped dillweed and lemon balm

¾ cup freshly grated Parmesan cheese

Boil the spaghetti in plenty of salted water until *al dente*.

Drain.

Melt the butter in a skillet and add the scallions.

Stir in the zest of lemon, sherry and *crème fraîche,* and cook for about 5 minutes.

Season with lemon juice, salt, and pepper to taste.

Mix the spaghetti well with the lemon sauce, dillweed, and lemon balm.

Serve sprinkled with Parmesan cheese.

Serves 4
Preparation time: 20 minutes
Calories per portion: 870
Recommended wine: Category **3** • **1** • or water

Recipes with
Herbs, Spices, and
Mushrooms

Dictionary of Ingredients

Bay leaves These come from the evergreen bay tree or bush. Used fresh, they are more aromatic (with a slight, very attractive bitterness) than when dried, the form in which they are most often used. Many cooks tend to use bay leaves too sparingly, a quarter or a half leaf at a time. It is better to use several leaves, which will produce a completely different, more integrated flavor. Unfortunately, fresh leaves are not always available, so it is a good idea to grow your own plant. Dried leaves should be green, not gray-brown.

Capers These are the flower buds of a Mediterranean shrub that grows on very dry rocks or walls. The smaller they are, the more subtle the flavor. The fresh buds have a very bitter taste and must be preserved, first in salt (they can be bought like this in some shops), then in vinegar.

Cèpes Fresh cèpes are best, but dried ones are excellent for sauces. Connoisseurs relish large, mature summer cèpes in sauces served with pasta; they have a more intense flavor than the small firm cèpes, which are better eaten raw or lightly fried.

Chanterelles These distinctive yellow fungi should be small and firm, with an inward-turning brim. Soft, funnel-shaped ones become rather tough when cooked because they release too much liquid and then boil, instead of frying or stewing gently.

Chervil A subtle herb that is at its most aromatic in spring and autumn. It is good only when used fresh and loses its flavor in prolonged cooking.

Chili peppers There are many varieties. Generally, you can say that the smaller they are, the hotter they are. Fresh chilies are the spiciest. When they are dried, the hotness may predominate, and pods harvested when mature often taste a bit floury and stale, so use only bright-red dried chilies that have been picked young. Preserved chilies – the proper Italian name is *peperoncini* – are best used straight out of the jar with cold meats and ham, but are not so good for cooking. They can easily give warm dishes an unpleasantly sour flavor. Colors range from bright green to dark green and from yellowy-orange to deep purple-red, but are no guide to how hot they are. Nonetheless, green chilies usually still have a slight taste of sweet peppers, while red ones have lost this characteristic.

Chives These taste nice only when they are fresh, which is not a problem in temperate climates, where they are always available. Do not cook them with food; add them raw at the last moment.

Coriander leaves Often called Chinese parsley or *cilantro*, they have a peculiar, powerful aroma that is not to everyone's taste. They should only be used fresh, and can easily be grown from coriander seeds.

Curry powder A mixture of spices originating from Asia that can vary greatly according to the dish in which it is used. When the British went to India they were so delighted with the practical application of the powders or pastes made from mixed spices that they immediately produced a standard mixture. Turmeric, which gives a yellow color, generally predominates in this, supplemented by every conceivable tropical flavoring. Make sure you buy good-quality curry powder.

Dillweed A herb that originated in northern Europe. It is suitable only for pasta dishes that do not originate from the Mediterranean area.

Fennel The leaves cut from the root bulb are a good herb with fish, and the seed can also be used with vegetable and meat dishes. The bulb can be cooked too.

Ginger An aromatic root that is best used fresh in small quantities. It keeps well in the vegetable compartment of a refrigerator if it stays moist. If you use ginger only occasionally, you can use the powdered version.

Ground red pepper (cayenne) This is made from ground red chilies, and is particularly hot and aromatic. It quickly loses its spicy flavor, but retains its nip.

Lemon balm An old medicinal and culinary herb with a marked lemon aroma. The fresh, raw leaves are always to be preferred to dried ones.

Marjoram A classic herb used to flavor soups and braised meats. Be careful not to add too much. Dried marjoram is also good.

Morels These spring mushrooms have, unfortunately, become rare and expensive, but are available dried. There are gray-brown, longish, pointed morels, and rounder, yellowish, field morels. Dried imported morels from the Himalayas are relatively good value, not to be confused with the completely different, cheap Chinese morels. Always wash morels thoroughly and, when soaking, allow time for them to swell fully.

Mushrooms There are many completely different kinds of mushroom. The commonest is the white cultivated mushroom, which was developed from the field mushroom and has a very mild flavor. The brown-skinned variety, developed from wood mushrooms, is stronger, and the gray-brown *champignon de Paris* is best of all. Wild varieties always have a stronger flavor than cultivated mushrooms.

Oregano A wild relation of marjoram, it is a prolific perennial, normally used dried. A related form of wild marjoram grows in temperate climates, but it does not have the pungency of the "pizza herb" oregano, and can be rather like mint.

Oyster mushrooms When they are fairly young, they are tender with a mild flavor almost like wild angelica, but as they get older they can have a pungent flavor and may be tough. The stalks should always be discarded.

Paprika This comes in varying degrees of hotness: the more seeds and internal membranes are ground up with the dried flesh of the peppers, the hotter the flavor and the brighter the color. The label usually indicates mild, sweet or hot. The mild, sweet varieties turn to sugar easily, so be careful when frying it that the powder does not burn.

Pepper A universal seasoning, which should always be of the finest quality. Good pepper has a marked spiciness combined with its hotness. White pepper is mild and gentle, while black pepper gives more background flavor and is more fiery. Green peppers, berries that have been harvested before they are ripe, have a "green" aroma; they are best fresh, but are also good in brine or freeze-dried. So-called "red pepper" is not a true pepper, coming from the elder family. Along with its peppery taste, it has a tantalizing exotic spiciness.

Rosemary The firm needles of this strongly scented evergreen bush give off a resinous, spicy aroma. Use liberally only with meat. Dries well.

Saffron The stigmas of the special sort of crocus from which saffron is produced are exceptionally laborious to collect, so saffron is the most expensive of all the spices. Therefore there are lots of counterfeits – based for example, on marigold petals – which are impossible to detect in powdered saffron. It is preferable to buy whole strands of saffron so as to be able to savor the full, round flavor of this spice properly. It colors sauces and soups a golden yellow.

Sage The silvery leaves of this perennial shrub need fat to enable them to divulge their full aroma. Do not be too stingy –fresh or dried sage can be used with everything.

Savory The young leaves of summer savory in particular have a strong peppery flavor. Perennial winter savory, known in French as *sariette*, is even more intense. It is at its most aromatic just as it is starting to bloom, and can be successfully dried when it is at that stage.

Thyme Common garden thyme has small bright green leaves, red on the underside, and a pleasant, mild aroma. Provençal thyme with tiny, hard, silvery leaves, is much more pungent and subtle. Wild or creeping thyme grows in dry areas in temperate climates, but the powerfully scented lemon thyme is less common. Many people prefer dried thyme to fresh because it is less bitter.

Turmeric Related to ginger, but less aromatic and somewhat bitter, turmeric is a powerful dye, noted for its yellow color.

Spinach taglierini with fresh herbs

1 lb. spinach taglierini
salted water
½–⅝ cup olive oil
1 bunch scallions, washed and sliced
2 cloves garlic, finely chopped
1½ cups freshly chopped herbs, e.g. summer savory, marjoram, basil, parsley, tarragon, chives, thyme, or lemon balm
salt
freshly ground pepper
¾ cup freshly grated Parmesan cheese or pecorino cheese

Cook the pasta in plenty of salted water until *al dente*.

Drain.

Heat the oil in a large skillet, and gently fry the scallions and garlic until they are transparent.

Add the pasta to the pan and heat through.

Mix in the fresh, chopped herbs.

Season with salt and pepper to taste.

Serve sprinkled with grated cheese.

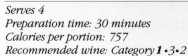

Serves 4
Preparation time: 30 minutes
Calories per portion: 757
Recommended wine: Category 1•3•2

Spaghetti with basil and pine nuts

4 bunches basil

4 cloves garlic, peeled and coarsely chopped

½ cup pine nuts, finely chopped

½ teaspoon coarse sea salt

⅝ cup olive oil

1 cup grated pecorino cheese

1 cup grated Parmesan cheese

freshly ground pepper

1 lb. spaghetti

salted water

Pick over the basil, wash it carefully, and use paper towels to dry it; remove the stems and coarsely chop the leaves.

Pound the basil in a mortar with the garlic, pine nuts, and sea salt; mix in ⅓ cup of pecorino cheese, then ⅓ cup of Parmesan.

Stir the olive oil into this thick paste (pesto) until it reaches a creamy consistency, then season with pepper.

Cook the spaghetti in plenty of salted water until *al dente*.

Drain and reserve the cooking water.

Mix 2–3 tablespoons of the water into the pesto.

Mix the spaghetti with the pesto.

Pass around the remaining pecorino and Parmesan cheese mixed together in a bowl.

Serves 4
Preparation time: 40 minutes
Calories per portion: 964
Recommended wine: Category **1**•**4**•**2**

Bucatini with oyster mushrooms

¼ lb. slab bacon, diced (about ⅔ cup)

⅜ cup olive oil

2 cloves garlic, peeled and sliced

1½ lb. oyster mushrooms, cleaned (not washed)

1 lb. ripe tomatoes, peeled, quartered and deseeded

salt

freshly ground pepper

sprigs of fresh thyme or ½ teaspoon dried thyme

1–2 teaspoons lemon juice

14 oz. bucatini

salted water

1 cup freshly grated Parmesan cheese or pecorino cheese

Heat the bacon in a skillet, stirring it until the fat begins to run, then remove and reserve.

Remove the hard stalks from the mushrooms and discard.

Put the oil and garlic into the skillet, add the mushrooms and fry briskly.

Add the tomatoes and season with salt, pepper, and thyme.

Continue cooking over a low heat in the uncovered pan until all the ingredients are done.

Add lemon juice to taste and return the bacon to the mixture.

Cook the bucatini in plenty of salted water until *al dente*.

Drain.

Mix the pasta with the mushroom and bacon sauce, arrange on a dish, and serve sprinkled with cheese.

Serves 4
Preparation time: 40 minutes
Calories per portion: 869
Recommended wine: Category **4** • **3** • **5**

Spaghetti with chanterelles

4 tablespoons butter

1 onion, peeled and diced

1 lb. fresh chanterelles, cleaned and cut into large chunks

salt

freshly ground pepper

1 clove garlic, crushed

2 tablespoons water

14 oz. spinach spaghetti

salted water

2 tablespoons finely chopped parsley

Melt the butter in a skillet, add the onion and cook until transparent.

Add the chanterelles, fry, then season with salt, pepper, and the garlic.

Add 2 tablespoons water, cover and simmer over a low heat until ready.

Cook the spaghetti in plenty of salted water until *al dente*.

Drain.

Mix the spaghetti with the chanterelles and the parsley, and serve.

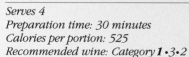

Serves 4
Preparation time: 30 minutes
Calories per portion: 525
Recommended wine: Category **1**•3•2

60

Spaghetti with cèpes

4 tablespoons butter

1 lb. small (if possible) cèpes, cleaned and cut into thin slices

salt

freshly ground pepper

12 oz. spaghetti

salted water

1 bunch flat-leaf parsley, finely chopped

Melt the butter in a skillet and fry the cèpes, seasoning with salt and pepper.

Meanwhile cook the spaghetti in plenty of salted water until *al dente*.

Drain.

Mix the cèpes with the spaghetti.

Sprinkle with parsley and serve.

Serves 4 as a starter
Preparation time: 20 minutes
Calories per portion: 455.5
Recommended wine: Category **3 • 2 • 1**

Taglierini with butter and truffles

14 oz. fresh taglierini

salted water

½ cup butter

⅜ cup broth or white wine

salt

freshly ground pepper

1 white truffle, cleaned with a fine
   brush

¼ cup very finely grated pecorino
   cheese

Cook the taglierini in plenty of salted
water until *al dente*.

Drain, and empty into a preheated
bowl.

Melt the butter in a small pan, add
the broth or white wine.

Pour this sauce over the taglierini,
mix, and season with salt and
pepper.

Divide the pasta onto 4 plates.

Use a mushroom slice to pare slivers
of the truffle over the pasta.

Serve sprinkled with cheese.

Serves 4
Preparation time: 10–15 minutes
Calories per portion: 706
Recommended wine: Category **1**•4•2

Recipes with Cheese and Cream

Dictionary of Ingredients

Bel Paese A semi-hard cheese from Lombardy with a 45–52 percent fat content. A whole cheese weighs about 4½ lb., and can be cut into slices about 8 in. thick. It should have a thin, smooth, yellow crust, and the cheese itself should be soft, creamy, and ivory-colored. It is made from whole pasteurized milk, so the same quality can be achieved throughout the year. It is especially good as an *au gratin* topping.

Blue-veined cheese A semi-hard cheese with an internal blue mold, usually with a 40-45 percent fat content; see Gorgonzola.

Caciocavallo This literally means "rider's cheese". It is a hard cheese made from cow's milk, softened with hot water to make it pliable so that it can be molded into the characteristic, pear-shaped cake. Often it is also smoked, and whole cheeses weigh from 4½ to 7 lb. Originally it came from Sicily, but it is now available throughout Italy. The cheese is hung on a string and the flavor develops as it matures; after two to four months it can be served as dessert cheese. It should be grated.

There is also a caciocavallo cheese made from a combination of cow's and sheep's milk.

Cream cheese, curd cheese or **farmer's cheese** Seldom used in cooking, but can be substituted for ricotta.

Fontina This full-fat hard cheese made from cow's milk melts easily, and becomes smooth and runny when heated. Therefore it is used in cooking, particularly for sauces, fondues, and *au gratin* toppings. Its fat content is at least 45 percent. A whole cheese is cylindrical in form, and weighs from 16 to 21 lb. It has a thick, hard, light-brown rind, and the cheese itself is straw-colored and rubbery with a few small holes.

It is produced only in the Aosta valley, and the best cheeses are made in summer from milk produced on mountain pastures. Old Fontina is also suitable for grating.

Gorgonzola A blue-veined cheese from Lombardy, also now produced in Piedmont, made from whole milk with a fat content of at least 48 percent. The cheeses are pressed in cylindrical molds of varying sizes, matured for at least two months, and weigh from 13 to 28 lb. The rind is rough and reddish in color; the cheese itself varies from white to pale yellow, with veins of blue mold running through it. It has a strong flavor, but it should not be too powerful if it is being heated to serve with pasta – the younger the better in this case! Gorgonzola must always be kept wrapped in silver paper. Gorgonzola "layered" with mascarpone or seasoned with basil cream is also available.

Grana Padano This large, cylindrical, bulging cheese, which weighs from 52 to 88 lb., is matured for at least six months, ideally for twenty-four. It is grated, and is similar to Parmigiano Reggiano.

Gruyère An ivory-colored full-fat hard cheese with small holes and developing cracks as it ages. It comes from Switzerland and France. It is good for flavoring and for toppings.

Hard cheese Hard cheeses tend to crumble when sliced or cut, and often have cracks. In many kinds you can still discern the actual curd where the crack has occurred.

Mascarpone A farmer's cheese with a high cream and high-fat content. It is slightly sour and can be used both for pasta dishes and desserts.

Mozzarella A full-fat farmer's cheese which can be preserved only in a brine, mozzarella was originally made from buffalo milk; nowadays it is made mainly from cow's milk, or from a mixture of the two. The curd is rubbery, white in color, and melts easily. It has a slightly tart, refreshing taste and is excellent on pizzas and as a topping on vegetables.

Parmesan cheese See p. 32.

Pecorino This name alone means only a sheep's-milk cheese. The word indicating its place of origin is the key to a specific type of cheese.

Pecorino Romano Italy's oldest cheese, Romano is a half-fat cheese suitable for slicing. It is cylindrical in shape, weighs between 17 and 64 lb., and has a fat content of at least 30 percent. The rind is dark brown; the cheese itself is hard, grainy, and whitish to straw-colored. It has a piquant, slightly sharp taste. It grates well.

Pecorino Sardo or **Fiore Sardo** A hard cheese, with a fat content at least 40 percent. It weighs between 3 and 8 lb., and is cylindrical or cone-shaped. The rind is yellow to dark brown and the cheese light to yellowish, with a piquant, slightly sour taste, which becomes stronger after the cheese has been stored for six months. It is then ideal for grating and for pesto (a sauce based on basil).

Pecorino Siciliano A hard cheese with a fat content of at least 40 percent. It, too, is used for grating.

Pecorino Toscano This cheese weighs between 2 and 5 lb. and has an elongated shape. It is often eaten fresh, and is used like Pecorino Romano.

Provolone A hard cheese made from cow's milk, with a 45 percent fat content. Italy's most popular cheese, it comes in every conceivable shape and size, always tied up with string so that it can be hung up. It is sometimes smoked. When it is young, one or two months old, it has a mild, sweetish taste; after four months it is buttery and spicy; after six months it is really sharp, and then it is good for grating.

Ricotta The name means "recooked" and refers to the fact that ricotta is made from the whey (from cow's or sheep's milk) left over after making another cheese. The whey is slowly heated, the protein flocculates and is strained off. The curd cheese left behind is then pressed into a variety of shapes. It is an indispensable ingredient in fillings for pasta.

Robiola A full-fat farmer's cheese, usually made from a combination of cow's and goat's or sheep's milk, and more rarely from pure goat's milk. The cheeses weigh from 9 to 14 oz., and are pure white with a delicately sourish, spicy, yet mild flavor.

Semi-hard cheese Soft but not runny, can be sliced, but not thinly.

Sheep's-milk cheese See Pecorino.

Slicing cheese Suitable for cutting into thin slices, with a typical fat content of between 30 and 60 percent.

Soft cheese Cheese that cannot be sliced, with a fat content generally between 20 and 60 percent, such as Camembert.

Swiss cheese Originating from Emmental in Switzerland, this cheese has conquered the world. A hard cheese made from whole cow's milk with a fat content of at least 45 percent, its characteristic feature is its holes, varying from the size of a cherry to that of a plum. The cheese itself is cream-colored, with a mild, almost sweetish aroma. It is the ideal cheese – equally good on its own and in cooking or roasted.

Taglierini with fondue sauce

14 oz. fontina or Swiss cheese

⅞ cup tepid milk

3 tablespoons butter

4 egg yolks

salt

freshly ground pepper

14 oz. taglierini

salted water

1 white truffle, cleaned with a brush

Slice the cheese thinly or cut it into small dice, place it in a bowl and pour the milk over it. Leave to steep for a few hours at least, ideally overnight.

Melt the butter in a small non-stick saucepan and add the milk with the softened cheese.

Place the pan with its contents in a double-boiler and melt to a smooth cream, stirring constantly with a spoon.

Gradually add the egg yolks, stirring hard the whole time until you have a thick creamy sauce.

Season with salt and pepper to taste.

Cook the taglierini in plenty of salted water until *al dente*.

Drain, then turn into a bowl.

Pour the fondue sauce over the pasta and carefully mix together.

Divide the pasta onto 4 plates, pare thin slivers of truffle over each, and serve immediately.

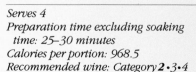

Serves 4

Preparation time excluding soaking time: 25–30 minutes

Calories per portion: 968.5

Recommended wine: Category 2 • 3 • 4

Spaghetti with Gorgonzola sauce

14 oz. spaghetti

salted water

7 oz. Gorgonzola, crumbled

1 tablespoon green peppercorns, fresh
or preserved

1 teaspoon dried sage leaves

1 cup light cream

1 tablespoon brandy

4 teaspoons butter, melted

salt

ground red pepper

Cook the spaghetti in plenty of salted water until *al dente*.

Put the Gorgonzola, peppercorns, and sage into a saucepan with the cream, cook on a low heat, stirring till creamy, then flavor with the brandy.

Drain the spaghetti, then toss it in butter.

Combine the Gorgonzola sauce with the buttered spaghetti, season with salt, and serve sprinkled with plenty of ground red pepper.

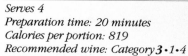

Serves 4
Preparation time: 20 minutes
Calories per portion: 819
Recommended wine: Category **3**•1•4

Spaghetti with mascarpone

1 lb. spinach spaghetti

salted water

3 tablespoons butter, melted

8 oz. mascarpone cheese

salt

freshly ground pepper

⅝ cup finely diced lean ham

½ cup freshly grated Parmesan cheese

Cook the spaghetti in plenty of salted water until *al dente*.

Drain.

Put the pasta mixed with the butter in a preheated bowl, and mix in the mascarpone.

Season with salt and pepper.

Serve sprinkled with the ham and Parmesan cheese.

Serves 4
Preparation time: 20 minutes
Calories per portion: 917
Recommended wine: Category 1•3•2

Bucatini with mozzarella

14 oz. bucatini

salted water

5 tablespoons butter, melted

½ cup freshly grated Parmesan cheese

salt

freshly ground pepper

½ cup light cream

7 oz. mozzarella cheese, thinly sliced

small piece of butter

1 tablespoon grated Parmesan cheese

basil leaves to garnish

Cook the bucatini in plenty of salted water until *al dente*.

Drain.

Mix the pasta with the butter, ½ cup Parmesan cheese, pepper, salt, and cream, and turn into an ovenproof dish.

Arrange the sliced mozzarella on top, dot with butter and sprinkle with Parmesan cheese.

Bake in the oven at 350°F until the cheese begins to melt.

Garnish with a few basil leaves and serve.

Serves 4
Preparation time: 35-40 minutes
Calories per portion: 835
Recommended wine: Category **3**•1•5

Spaghetti with mozzarella cheese and fresh tomatoes

1½ lb. ripe tomatoes, peeled

½–⅝ cup olive oil

a few sprigs of basil

1 teaspoon dried oregano

1½–2 tablespoons freshly grated
  Parmesan cheese

1 tablespoon small capers

1 tablespoon balsamic vinegar or
  lemon juice

½ teaspoon salt

freshly ground pepper

1 lb. spaghetti

7 oz. mozzarella cheese, thinly sliced

Break up the tomatoes with your fingers and remove the seeds.

Mix the tomatoes with the olive oil, basil leaves, oregano, Parmesan cheese and capers.

Add the vinegar or lemon juice, then salt and pepper to taste.

Cook the spaghetti in plenty of salted water until *al dente*.

Drain.

Serve in a bowl with the tomato sauce and slices of mozzarella cheese.

Serves 4
Preparation time: 30 minutes
Calories per portion: 945
Recommended wine: Category 1·3·2

Spaghetti with Parmesan cheese

1 lb. spaghetti or taglierini

salted water

1½ cups freshly grated Parmesan cheese

10 tablespoons (1¼ sticks) butter

freshly ground pepper

Cook the spaghetti or taglierini in plenty of salted water until *al dente*.

Drain, turn into a bowl, and mix quickly with the Parmesan cheese.

Cut the butter into small pieces and mix in.

Divide the pasta onto preheated plates, sprinkle with freshly ground pepper, and serve immediately. (You have to work quickly so that the spaghetti does not get cold.)

Variation

Instead of butter use cream.

Serves 4
Preparation time: 20 minutes
Calories per portion: 931
*Recommended wine: Category **1**•3•4*

Tomato spaghetti with pecorino cheese, mint, and pine nuts

1 lb. tomato spaghetti

salted water

⅜ cup olive oil

3 cloves garlic, finely chopped

⅝ cup pine nuts

2 bunches mint, cut into thin strips

salt

freshly ground pepper

4 oz. pecorino cheese, thinly sliced

Cook the tomato spaghetti in plenty of salted water until *al dente*.

Drain.

Heat the olive oil in a large skillet.

Brown the garlic and pine nuts in the oil.

Add half of the mint and all of the pasta.

Heat the whole mixture, turning as you do so, and season with salt and pepper.

Mix in half of the cheese, then divide into individual servings.

Serve sprinkled with the remaining cheese and mint.

Serves 4
Preparation time: 35 minutes
Calories per portion: 848
Recommended wine: Category 3•4•1

Spaghetti with pecorino cheese

1 lb. spaghetti

salted water

³⁄₈ cup olive oil

1 clove garlic, sliced

1 teaspoon dried mixed herbs

1 teaspoon preserved peppercorns

2 cups pecorino cheese, finely crumbled

Cook the spaghetti in plenty of salted water until *al dente*.

Drain.

Gently heat the olive oil in a saucepan.

Add the garlic and herbs, and fry gently for a short time.

Add the spaghetti and peppercorns, and mix well.

Mix in the cheese and serve.

Serves 4
Preparation time: 20 minutes
Calories per portion: 786
Recommended wine: Category 3•4•1

Spaghetti with four kinds of cheese

3½ cups all-purpose flour

4 eggs

2 tablespoons oil

1 teaspoon salt

1 teaspoon dried thyme

1 teaspoon dried mixed Italian herbs

salted water

½ cup butter, melted

½ cup freshly grated Parmesan cheese

½ cup freshly grated Fontina

½ cup freshly grated Provolone

½ cup freshly grated Swiss cheese

½ cup pasta cooking water or white wine

freshly ground pepper

1 tablespoon finely chopped parsley

Mix the flour with the eggs, oil, salt, and herbs, and knead until you have a firm dough.

Cover and leave to rest for 30 minutes.

Roll out using a pasta machine and turn through the spaghetti cutters.

Cook in plenty of salted water until *al dente*.

Drain.

Turn the spaghetti into a preheated bowl, and pour the melted butter and the cooking water or wine over it.

Mix all four grated cheeses into the spaghetti until they melt and begin to form strings.

Serve sprinkled with pepper and parsley.

Serves 4
Preparation time: 40 minutes
Calories per portion: 950
Recommended wine: Category 3·1·4

Spaghetti with Fish and Shellfish

Dictionary of Ingredients

All fish can, of course, be combined with spaghetti in some form. Even a small fish is enough to supplement a pasta dish. However, there are some types of fish that are used more often than others. This is to an extent dependent on fashion, but it is also a question of convenience: if the preparation of the fish or seafood for the sauce takes no longer than the time the spaghetti needs to cook, then you can really prepare a quick meal. Or perhaps you need only to open a can, or cut fish already dressed by the fishmonger into strips.

Anchovies Buy these small fish fresh when you can. If you buy them frozen, let them thaw in the refrigerator, then fillet or clean them. When buying salted anchovies, take care and buy good-quality ones; excellent Italian anchovies are generally available in large jars, and are usually better and cheaper than those in the small cans.

Caviar Price-wise this is at the opposite end of the spectrum from spaghetti, so select it carefully. If possible, buy caviar that is already opened and sample it before buying. Caviar should taste full and round, mild and succulent; it should not be too salty nor sour, and it should never suggest stale fish. Beluga caviar, with its large eggs, is the most expensive and looks the most impressive nestling in the spaghetti, but sevruga and ossietre can be equally delicious. Caviar heat-sealed in jars and small cans is pasteurized and does not have the same flavor. "Red caviar" (the roe from salmon) from Canada or Alaska in particular is sometimes very salty because it is intended to keep for a long time.

Clams Clean and cook fresh clams like mussels. Canned ones need just to be heated.

Crayfish

The brook crayfish is undoubtedly the finest of the various types. The pond crayfish, is an olive-gray color and has a less delicate flavor. To enhance its flavor you should always roast the shell, dowse it with some wine and keep basting the crayfish with this liquor as cooking proceeds.

Langoustines These well-known crustaceans have long pincers that contain very little edible material and are bright pink in color. Their meat is tender and exceptionally delicious, but it is also very easily damaged. Any that are not completely fresh and impeccably chilled on ice can easily become woolly when they are cooked. Because they are so highly prized, other less tasty, and much cheaper, creatures with very loose-textured meat, such as shrimp tails (which end in a point, not in a broad tail like langoustines) and the short tails of Chilean langostinos, are often passed off as langoustines.

Mussels These must be fresh and not too big. Clean the mussels in bowls of cold water, scrubbing the shells. Discard any broken or open shells that do not close when tapped sharply. Always cook mussels very briefly, just until they open, and discard any shells that do not open when cooked.

Oysters Flat oysters undoubtedly have the best flavor. Oysters must be completely fresh, always closed, filled with their own water, alive, with a fresh smell of the sea. Never do more than heat them through – they become tough if boiled.

Salmon Salmon, an aristocrat among fish that used to be only available in the wild, is now farmed. The flesh should be firm, with a little fat running through it, but not too much. The color of farmed salmon is controlled by what the fish are fed on (the shells of crustaceans), so it is no guide to quality.

Sardines You can buy sardines fresh or canned. The best canned sardines in oil use olive oil.

Scallops The firm yet tender flesh and the delicate roe, known as the coral, have always had a special appeal for the gourmet and inspired exquisite creations from chefs. If you buy fresh scallops, choose ones that look whitish and have a bright orange coral. Make sure they have had the black vein removed and are ready to cook. Frozen scallops are rarely as tender as fresh ones.

Seaweed A plant that loves saline soil and likes salt water. The brilliant green members as thick as a knitting needle look like thin green beans. The plant has a salty, markedly sea-clean taste and looks pretty. If the tips of the strands are red, take care: only young plants are tender; older ones, which have absorbed more sun, are stringy.

Dried seaweed must be soaked or steamed, and it, too, has a strong flavor of the sea.

Shrimp There is an almost incredible variety of shrimp, fresh and frozen. Frozen shrimp are available cooked or raw. Choose tightly packed raw shrimp without frost; precooked shrimp can become tough when reheated.

Smoked salmon Use only top quality, as any potential defect is magnified when it is heated. Good smoked salmon is not too fatty, has a texture that is firm yet tender, should be moist but never soft and soggy, and is never cheap.

Snails The edible snail is available in cans. Buy them in a plain liquid,

not in a prepared sauce.

Squid Squid, or calamari, are generally available frozen. You must thaw frozen squid slowly in the refrigerator and cook it briefly; if it is not correctly thawed or is overcooked, it will become tough. Octopus is delicious, too: if you can get young ones, known to the Italians as *moscardini*, snatch them up.

Tuna Although fresh tuna is available, the recipe in this book calls for canned tuna. You can buy canned tuna that has been preserved in various kinds of oil or in brine.

Spaghettini with oysters

16 oysters

2 oz. slab bacon, finely diced

1 shallot, finely chopped

1½ tablespoons butter

½ cup dry white wine

2 tablespoons dry vermouth

1 small package of saffron strands

3/8 cup light cream

1 bunch scallions, finely chopped

2 cloves garlic, crushed

2 tablespoons olive oil

1 lb. spinach, washed and scalded with
 salted water

salt

freshly ground pepper

10 oz. spaghettini

salted water

Remove the oysters from their shells
and reserve the liquid.

Gently fry the bacon and the shallot
in the butter until they are
transparent, add the wine and cook
until reduced by half.

Add the vermouth, saffron, cream,
oysters, and oyster liquid, and cook
until the edges of the oysters start to
curl; set on one side.

Fry the scallions and garlic gently in
the oil.

Add the spinach and cook covered
for 5 minutes; season with salt and
pepper.

Meanwhile cook the spaghettini in
plenty of salted water until *al dente*.

Drain.

Mix the pasta with the spinach and
serve with the oyster sauce.

Serves 4 as an appetizer
Preparation time: 55 minutes
Calories per portion: 677
Recommended wine: Category 2·1·6

Spaghetti with crayfish in orange butter

2 cups flour

1 egg

2 egg yolks

½ teaspoon salt

1 shallot, finely diced

¾ cup butter

1 cup freshly squeezed orange juice

a few sprigs tarragon

4 teaspoons dry vermouth

¼ cup light cream

salt

freshly ground pepper

a pinch of ground red pepper

4 teaspoons cognac

12 crayfish, cooked and removed from their shells

2 oranges, peeled and divided into segments

1½ tablespoons butter, melted

Work the flour, egg, egg yolks, and salt into a firm dough, cover and leave to rest for 30 minutes.

Roll out briefly on a floured work surface, then use a pasta machine to make the pasta (see p. 13).

Melt 1½ tablespoons of butter in a skillet and fry the shallot until it is transparent.

Add the orange juice, tarragon, and vermouth, and boil until the liquid is reduced by half.

Strain the sauce, gradually beat in the remaining butter in small pieces, and add the cream.

Season with salt, pepper, and ground red pepper; add the cognac, crayfish and orange segments and keep warm.

Cook the spaghetti in plenty of salted water until *al dente*, then drain and toss the pasta in the melted butter.

Divide the spaghetti onto 4 plates, pour the orange butter on top, and garnish with the pincers and tails.

Serves 4 as an appetizer
Preparation time: 50 minutes
Calories per portion: 791
Recommended wine: Category 2 • 6 • 1

Spaghetti with shrimp

5 tablespoons olive oil

2 tablespoons butter

3 cloves garlic, finely chopped

1 bunch scallions, washed and
   chopped into fine rings

¼ teaspoon curry powder

¼ cup dry sherry

1 cup dry white wine

a handful of finely chopped leaves of
   fresh herbs such as marjoram,
   thyme or mint

2½ cups peeled shrimps

salt

freshly ground pepper

14 oz. spaghetti

salted water

1 tablespoon finely chopped fresh
   dillweed

Heat 3 tablespoons of olive oil and
the butter in a large skillet.

Fry the garlic and scallions until soft.

Stir in the curry powder, sherry,
wine, and herbs.

Add the shrimp, cover and simmer
gently, adding salt and pepper to
taste.

Meanwhile cook the spaghetti in a
large pot of salted water until *al
dente.*

Drain, then mix with the remaining
olive oil.

Divide the spaghetti onto plates,
pour on the shrimp sauce, sprinkle
with dillweed, and serve.

Serves 4
Preparation time: 30 minutes
Calories per portion: 775
Recommended wine: Category 2 • 1 • 3

Spaghetti with scallops

12 large scallops, washed and cleaned,
     or 10 oz. frozen scallop meat

juice of 1 lemon

freshly ground pepper

4 teaspoons dry sherry

4 teaspoons Marsala

3 tablespoons butter

2 scallions, finely chopped

1 clove garlic, crushed

1 small package powdered saffron

1 cup light cream

a handful of chervil, roughly chopped

8 red peppercorns, crushed

14 oz. spaghetti

salted water

2 tablespoons butter, melted

freshly ground pepper

chervil leaves as garnish

Halve the scallops horizontally, and
marinate for 30 minutes in the lemon
juice, pepper, sherry, and Marsala.

Melt the butter in a skillet, and gently
fry the scallions and garlic until they
are transparent.

Add the scallops and the marinade,
and simmer on a low heat until
cooked.

Remove, stir in the saffron and
cream, and boil for 2 minutes.

Put the chervil, peppercorns, and
scallops in the skillet, cover and
leave to rest.

Cook the spaghetti in plenty of
boiling salted water until *al dente*,
then drain.

Mix the spaghetti with the melted
butter in a bowl.

Divide the spaghetti onto 4 plates,
put the scallops – 3 each – and the
sauce on top.

Serve with freshly ground pepper
and the chervil leaves scattered on
top.

Serves 4
Preparation time: 35 minutes
Calories per portion: 787
Recommended wine: Category 2.1.3

Spaghetti with caviar

12 oz. spaghetti

salted water

4 tablespoons butter

2 onions, finely chopped

2 cloves garlic, finely chopped

⅞ cup crème fraîche

⅜ cup spaghetti water or white wine

salt

freshly ground pepper

3 oz. black beluga caviar

Cook the spaghetti in plenty of salted water until *al dente*.

At the same time melt the butter in a skillet and fry the onion and garlic until transparent, then add the crème fraîche and spaghetti water or white wine.

Cook together for about 5 minutes.

Strain the sauce through a sieve.

Season sparingly with salt and pepper.

Drain the spaghetti.

Divide the spaghetti onto 4 plates, and put the sauce and caviar on top.

Serves 4
Preparation time: 20 minutes
Calories per portion: 676
Recommended wine: Category 6 • 2 • 1

Bucatini with mussels

2 onions, diced

2 cloves garlic, sliced

2 tablespoons oil

½ cup dry white wine

a few peppercorns

4½ pints mussels in their shells, scrubbed

2 sprigs parsley

2 tablespoons butter

1¼ cups thinly sliced carrots

2–3 leeks, washed and sliced in rings

salt, freshly ground pepper

¼ cup dry vermouth

1 tablespoon heavy cream

2 ripe tomatoes, peeled, deseeded and chopped

14 oz. bucatini

salted water

small bunch tarragon, with the leaves stripped from the stems

Gently fry the onions and garlic in the oil.

Add the wine, peppercorns, mussels, and parsley, then cover and simmer for about 5 minutes until the mussels open.

Drain the mussels and reserve the liquid; take three-quarters of the mussels out of the shells and reserve.

Melt the butter in a skillet and add the sliced carrots and leeks, the chopped tomatoes and the strained stock from the mussels.

Season with the salt and pepper, add the vermouth and heavy cream. and cook the vegetables until they are tender but still crisp.

Add the shelled and unshelled mussels and heat through.

Cook the pasta in plenty of salted water until *al dente*.

Drain, combine the bucatini and the mussels in a large bowl.

Serve sprinkled with tarragon.

Serves 4
Preparation time: 45 minutes
Calories per portion: 615
Recommended wine: Category 2•1•3

Spaghetti with smoked salmon

1 shallot, finely chopped
1 clove garlic, crushed
2 tablespoons butter
3 ripe tomatoes, peeled, deseeded and finely chopped
2 tablespoons brandy
2 tablespoons white wine
salt
freshly ground pepper
1¾ cups light cream
6 oz. smoked salmon, cut into thin strips
small bunch watercress, the leaves stripped from their stems
a few drops of lemon juice
14 oz. spaghetti or spaghettini
salted water

Fry the shallot and garlic in butter until they are transparent.

Add the tomatoes and stew for 5 minutes.

Add the brandy, wine, salt, pepper, and cream, and cook for 5 minutes, stirring constantly.

Put the smoked salmon and watercress into the hot sauce.

Meanwhile cook the spaghettini in plenty of salted water until *al dente*.

Drain the pasta and mix well with the sauce.

Serves 4
Preparation time: 30 minutes
Calories per portion: 883
Recommended wine: Category 2·1·6

Spaghetti with fried sardines

1 lb. fennel with its green leaves,
  cleaned and cut into ½-in. cubes

about 4 quarts salted water

½ cup olive oil

1 onion, finely chopped

4 anchovies, well rinsed

2 tablespoons raisins, soaked

2 tablespoons pine nuts, fried in a little
  butter

1 cup flour

¼ teaspoon salt

1 small package powdered saffron

1 lb. medium-size fresh sardines,
  boned and filleted

14 oz. spaghetti

freshly ground pepper

chopped fennel leaves

Cook the fennel in salted water until tender, then drain, reserving the cooking liquid.

Gently fry the onion in 4 tablespoons olive oil until it is transparent.

Add the anchovies and, using a fork, crush to a paste.

Stir in 2 tablespoons of the fennel cooking liquid and add the raisins and pine nuts.

Mix the flour with the salt and saffron, then roll the sardine fillets in it.

Heat the remaining olive oil in a skillet and fry the sardine fillets to a golden brown.

Cook the spaghetti in the remaining fennel cooking water until *al dente*, then drain.

In a large bowl combine the pasta with the anchovy sauce and fennel.

Divide the pasta onto 4 plates, add the sardines, and serve with a sprinkling of pepper and fennel leaves.

Serves 4
Preparation time: 50 minutes
Calories per portion: 974
Recommended wine: Category **2**•1•3

Spaghetti with tuna sauce

1 onion, finely diced

2 cloves garlic, finely chopped

¼ cup olive oil

1 lb. ripe tomatoes, peeled, deseeded and roughly cut up

1 teaspoon dried oregano

2 x 6½-oz. cans tuna, preserved in brine

1 tablespoon capers, rinsed

1 tablespoon each green and black olives, pitted and roughly chopped

salt

freshly ground pepper

1 tablespoon chopped parsley

1 lb. spaghetti

salted water

Gently fry the chopped onion and garlic in the olive oil until it is transparent.

Add the tomatoes and oregano, cover and simmer on a low heat for about 10 minutes.

Drain the tuna fish in a strainer, then break up roughly.

Add the capers, olives, and tuna to the tomato sauce, heat through, and season with salt, pepper, and parsley.

Cook the spaghetti in plenty of salted water until *al dente*.

Drain.

Divide the spaghetti onto 4 plates and pour the sauce over it. (Do not serve cheese with this dish.)

Serves 4
Preparation time: 35 minutes
Calories per portion: 843
Recommended wine: Category **1** • **2** • **3**

Spaghetti with squid in its own ink

1 lb. squid with ink-bags (or substitute
  2 oz. caviar, crushed, for the ink)

1 clove garlic, chopped

1 onion, chopped

¼ cup olive oil

1 cup dry white wine

salt

freshly ground pepper

1 small chili pepper, finely chopped

14 oz. spaghetti

salted water

2 tablespoons light cream

1 bunch parsley, chopped

Clean the squid, reserving the ink.
Cut the mouths off the heads, then
slice the squid into rings.

Fry the garlic and onion in the olive
oil until they are transparent.

Add the rings of squid and their
heads, the chili pepper, white wine
and seasoning.

Cover, simmer for 15–20 minutes,
then remove the squid using a
slotted spoon.

Meanwhile cook the spaghetti in
plenty of salted water until *al dente*.

Drain.

Stir the cream and ink (or caviar)
into the fish stock.

Put the spaghetti into the pan and
turn it to let it absorb the stock.

Mix the pieces of squid in with the
rest, divide onto individual plates,
and serve sprinkled with parsley.

Serves 4
Preparation time: 50 minutes
Calories per portion: 628
Recommended wine: Category **2**•1•6

Capellini with clams

4 pints fresh (or frozen) clams,
   thoroughly scrubbed

½ cup dry white wine

⅜ cup olive oil

2 shallots, finely diced

3 cloves garlic, peeled and finely
   chopped

1 bunch flat-leaf parsley, chopped

freshly ground pepper

1 lb. capellini

salted water

Cook the clams in the white wine
with the lid on until all the shells
have opened (discard any shells that
do not open).

Drain the clams in a sieve with a
bowl underneath to catch the liquid.

Heat the oil in a large pot and fry the
shallots and garlic until soft.

Add the clam broth to the pot and
boil until half the liquid has
evaporated.

Remove half of the clams from their
shells.

Add these and the clams still in their
shells to the broth, heat, then add
the parsley and season with pepper.

Meanwhile cook the capellini in
plenty of salted water until *al dente*.

Drain.

Mix the capellini with the clams and
sauce, sprinkle with pepper and
serve immediately.

Variation

Add 1 finely chopped fresh chili
pepper to the broth when returning
the shellfish to the pot.

Serves 4
Preparation time: 35-40 minutes
Calories per portion: 738
*Recommended wine: Category **2**•1•3*

Spaghetti with snails

1 onion, finely diced

1 clove garlic, finely chopped

2 oz. slab bacon, diced (about ⅓ cup)

1 tablespoon olive oil

¾ lb. ripe tomatoes, peeled, deseeded and diced

36 snails in their shells, stuffed with herb butter

1 cup dry white wine

1 cup chicken broth

4 teaspoons dry sherry

2 cups fresh mushrooms, cleaned and thinly sliced

½ teaspoon dried mixed herbs

salt

freshly ground pepper

small bunch parsley, chopped

1 lb. spaghetti or spaghettini

salted water

Fry the onions, garlic and bacon in the oil until transparent.

Add the tomatoes and cook gently.

Now add the snails in their shells, the white wine, broth and sherry, cover and simmer for 10 minutes.

Remove the snails from their shells.

Cook the mushrooms and herbs in the sauce for 10 minutes, return the snails, and season with salt, pepper, and the parsley.

Cook the spaghetti in plenty of salted water until *al dente*.

Drain.

Serve the spaghetti well mixed with the sauce.

Serves 4
Preparation time: 35 minutes
Calories per portion: 834
Recommended wine: Category **2** • **1** • **3**

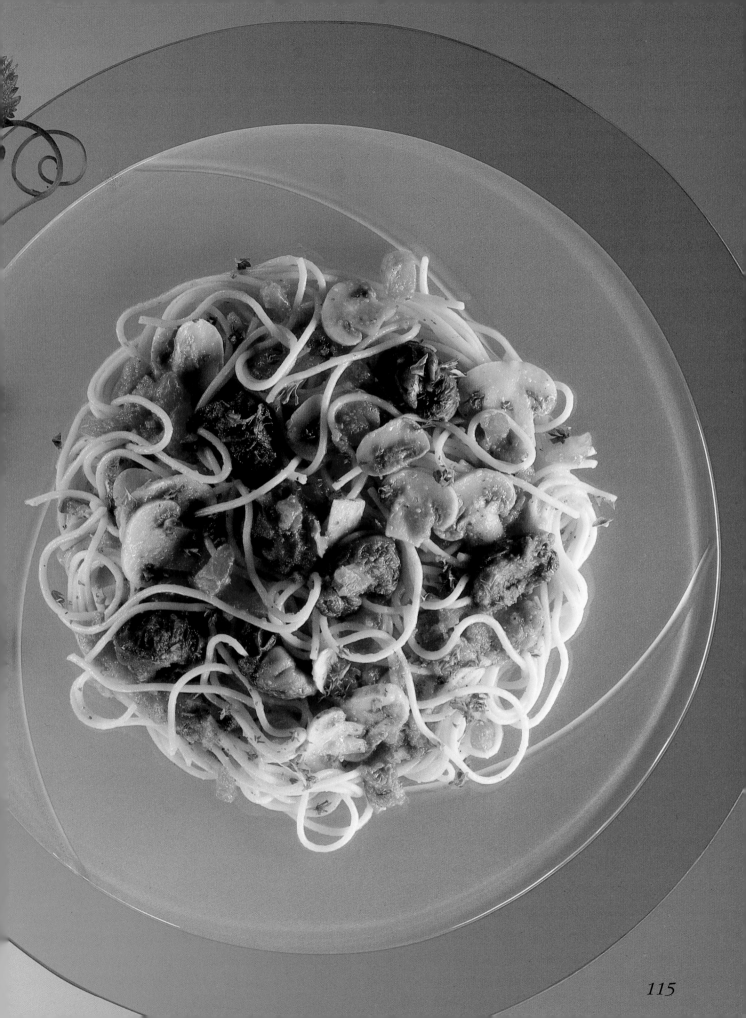

*Recipes with
Meat*

Dictionary of Ingredients

Bacon Most of the recipes in this book call for slab bacon, which can be diced. If you cannot find any, use sliced bacon cut into pieces.

Beef It should always be well hung and veined or marbled with fat. Choose the cut depending on how the meat is to be used.
The shorter the fibers and the less sinew the meat has, the more suitable it is for a quick cooking method such as frying or roasting. Such meat tends to come from parts the animal uses less for movement and work: the back and hindquarters. The meat from parts of the animal that get intensive use, such as the neck, forequarters and legs, has longer fibers and is full of sinews, which take a long time to become tender. Once tender, however, both they and the bones impart valuable flavoring elements to the surrounding flesh. For succulent braised dishes, slow-cooking stews and tasty sauces, you should use meat with a good deal of fat running through it.

It is best to grind beef yourself. Take a top round or rump roast, or brisket, carefully remove the gristle, and – depending on what you intend to make – grind once (for coarse-grained stuffings and sauces) or twice (for close-textured stuff-ings), using a fine cutter.

Bresaola A salted, air-dried beef from Italy.

Chicken In Italy chicken is still regarded as a delicacy, and consequently the birds are well tended and well fed. Hardly any are fed on concentrates; they are almost all raised on grain, especially corn, which shows in their yellow fat and yellow skin.

Chicken liver This too is highly prized, and coming from the birds described above is tasty, tender, light, and plump – far removed from the lean, dark liver from factory-farmed birds.

Coppa Pickle-cured, air-dried neck of pork, a speciality of the region of the River Po. Highly seasoned.

Cotecchino A spicy sausage, which should be boiled, an indispensable ingredient in *bollito misto* in particular. Chopped up, it can be used in any sauce.

Game Game occupies a special place in Italy. In every region there are distinctive sauces using the less expensive types of game, which go particularly well with pasta because they are highly seasoned. Wild boar and hare are the most common, and in the mountains chamois, too. Game birds other than ducks are seldom available. As a rule, all game is very well hung, so when it is cooked, seasoning in the form of wine, herbs, and spices is used liberally.

Ham In Italy only leg of pork may be called ham or a supplementary explanation has to be given. The home of spaghetti produces superb hams, the best of them made according to fixed rules with a strict checking procedure.

Parma ham must come from Parma, and the pigs must have been reared in the Parma area on special food. The ham is mild, not too salty and very aromatic. It matures in the clear air of the Parma hills.

San Daniele is a meaty ham, again mildly aromatic, from Friuli; its special character comes from the dry, clear air of the region.

Prosciutto del Veneto comes from Venice, and is steadily winning a reputation for superb quality.

Other dry-cured Italian hams,

generally referred to as *prosciutto,* can also be good. Cooked ham is also available in Italy, produced in much the same way as here, although it is sometimes a little more highly seasoned. In Italy ham is almost always cut from the bone. As it is the best quality and a certain amount of waste must be allowed for, the price is high.

Lamb The meat of sheep up to a year old can be sold as lamb. There is obviously a difference between the taste of a 6-month-old and a 12-month-old animal. The meat of lambs that have never grazed and been fed only on their mother's milk is fairly light-colored and tender with a flavor that is attractive though not powerful. The meat of lambs that have grazed is affected by the quality of their food: the sparser the pasture and the drier its fragrance, the stronger the flavor of the meat.

Mortadella A famous sausage made in Bologna, a triumph of sausage-making. The meat, fat and bacon, the seasoning and water content are so skillfully balanced that the huge sausages keep for a long time even without refrigeration. The original Italian mortadella is far superior to imitations produced under the same name.

Rabbit Tender, light meat that is equally good roasted and braised, rabbit is very popular in Italy, where excellent quality is available throughout the country at very reasonable prices. In America it still tends to be undervalued.

Salami Made from pork, this is the Italian sausage *par excellence.* The first syllable, 'sal', refers to the method of preservation: salt. There are many different kinds of salami, the best coming from Lombardy (Milan) and Emilia-Romagna. The taste depends on the size, origin, seasoning, and age.

Salsicce A small, dry-cured sausage with seasoning that varies from one area to another. They are often also sold fresh and used as a basis for pasta sauces.

Veal Italy's most popular meat, almost invariably of very high quality, as people are willing to pay for it and prefer to eat less rather than have a bigger helping of inferior meat.

Spaghetti with meat and tomato sauce

3 tablespoons olive oil

2 oz. raw ham, diced

1 small onion, diced

1 carrot, scrubbed and diced

¾ cup celery, washed and diced

2 cloves garlic, finely chopped

1 lb. ground beef

½ teaspoon each dried marjoram and thyme or 1 bunch each fresh marjoram and thyme (leaves stripped from stems)

1 tablespoon chopped parsley

salt

freshly ground pepper

½ cup dry red wine

1 x 14-oz. can peeled tomatoes, drained and deseeded

1 tablespoon tomato paste

1 lb. spaghetti

salted water

¾ cup freshly grated Parmesan cheese

Heat the oil in a deep skillet, add the ham, onion, carrot, celery, and garlic, and cook gently.

Add the ground beef and fry until it browns.

Add the herbs, salt, and pepper, cover with red wine, and cook until the wine has been absorbed.

Add the tomatoes and tomato paste, stir, crushing the tomatoes with the spoon.

Cook until the sauce is creamy, stirring from time to time.

Cook the spaghetti in plenty of salted water until *al dente*.

Drain.

Pour the sauce over the spaghetti and serve immediately. Pass around a bowl of grated Parmesan cheese.

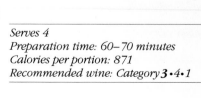

Serves 4
Preparation time: 60–70 minutes
Calories per portion: 871
Recommended wine: Category 3•4•1

Spaghetti with bacon, ham, and egg sauce

1 lb. spaghetti

salted water

1 rounded tablespoon butter

¼ lb. lean smoked slab bacon, diced
(about ⅔ cup)

⅓ cup diced cooked ham

3 egg yolks and 3 whole eggs

½ cup light cream

2 cloves garlic, crushed

¼ teaspoon salt

freshly ground pepper

½ cup grated Parmesan cheese

½ cup grated pecorino cheese

Cook the spaghetti in plenty of salted water until *al dente*.

Meanwhile melt the butter in a skillet and fry the diced bacon and ham in it.

Beat the eggs with the cream, garlic, salt, pepper, and cheese.

Drain the spaghetti.

Mix the pasta immediately with the beaten eggs, cream and cheese.

Add the bacon and ham, and mix in quickly. As the spaghetti is extremely hot, the eggs should set immediately without becoming lumpy.

Serve with a generous sprinkling of freshly ground pepper. (Leave people to add any extra salt they require at the table, as the bacon and ham are generally salty.)

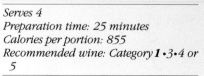

Serves 4
Preparation time: 25 minutes
Calories per portion: 855
Recommended wine: Category **1**•3•4 or
5

122

Taglierini with chicken liver

1 lb. taglierini

4½ pints chicken broth

2 onions, finely chopped

4½ tablespoons butter

small bunch sage leaves

1 lb. chicken liver, with any skin and
    sinews removed, roughly chopped

salt

freshly ground pepper

½ cup freshly grated Parmesan cheese

Cook the pasta in the boiling broth
until *al dente* – nearly all the broth
should be absorbed.

Fry the diced onion in butter until it
is golden.

Add the sage and chicken livers, and
cook until the livers begin to brown,
turning occasionally (the livers
should still be soft inside).

Season with salt and pepper.

Drain the taglierini.

Mix the pasta with the liver and
serve with Parmesan cheese.

Serves 4
Preparation time: 30 minutes
Calories per portion: 840
Recommended wine: Category 3•1•2

Capellini with snow peas and lamb

2 cloves garlic, finely chopped

1 oz. fresh ginger, peeled and finely chopped

¼ cup soy sauce

2 tablespoons dry sherry

1 teaspoon curry powder

2 teaspoons honey

½ teaspoon salt

¾ lb. lean boned lamb, cut in very thin strips ½ in. x 1½ in.

½ lb. young snow peas, washed, halved diagonally

1 bunch scallions, washed, cut slantwise into pieces ¾ in. long

5 tablespoons olive oil

½ cup chicken broth

salt

freshly ground pepper

1 lb. capellini

salted water

1 tablespoon fresh chopped coriander leaves (cilantro)

Mix together the first seven ingredients.

Place the lamb in the marinade and leave it for 1 hour.

Sauté the snow peas and scallions in hot oil, stirring all the time, then remove.

Drain the lamb, reserving the marinade, then fry it in the remaining oil.

Return the vegetables to the pan, add the chicken broth and the rest of the marinade, and season with salt and pepper.

Cook the capellini in plenty of salted water until *al dente*, then drain.

Fold the pasta into the meat and vegetable mixture, and serve sprinkled with coriander leaves.

Serves 4
Preparation time (not including marinading time): 40 minutes
Calories per portion: 768
Recommended wine: Category **5·4·3**

Spaghetti with peas and ham

2 tablespoons olive oil

2 tablespoons butter

1 bunch scallions, washed and finely diced

2½ cups shelled peas (frozen or fresh)

5 tablespoons cup meat bouillon (instant)

10 slices cooked ham, cut into ¼-in.-wide strips

salt

freshly ground pepper

1 tablespoon chopped parsley

1 lb. spaghetti

salted water

¾ cup Gruyère cheese, cut into small cubes

½ cup freshly grated Parmesan cheese

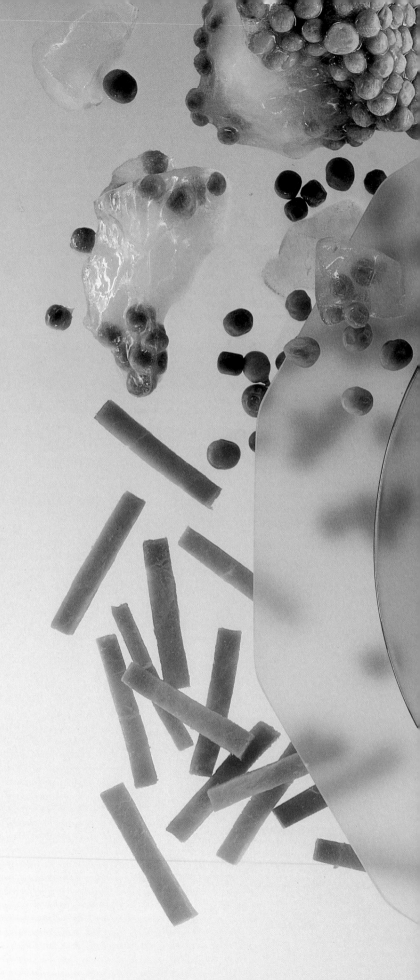

Heat the olive oil and 1 tablespoon of butter in a skillet and sauté the scallions until they are transparent.

Add the peas and meat bouillon, and cook over a moderate heat until soft.

In another skillet melt the remaining butter, add the ham and cook until lightly brown.

Add the ham to the peas and season with salt, pepper, and parsley.

Cook the spaghetti in plenty of salted water until *al dente*, then drain.

In a bowl combine the pasta with the pea and ham mixture and the cheese.

Mix again just before serving so that the cheese is properly melted.

Serves 4
Preparation time: 45 minutes
Calories per portion: 898
Recommended wine: Category 1·2·3

Spaghetti with fresh lima beans and prosciutto

⅓ cup olive oil
1 bunch scallions, cut into thin rings
3½ lb. fresh lima beans, shelled and skinned or 1 lb. frozen beans
⅓ cup broth
salt
freshly milled pepper
½ teaspoon dried thyme or freshly picked thyme leaves
1 lb. spaghetti
salted water
7 slices prosciutto cut into thin, narrow strips
¾ cup freshly grated Parmesan or pecorino cheese

Heat the olive oil in a skillet and fry the scallions until soft.

Add the beans and broth, season with salt, pepper and thyme, then cover and cook for about 15 minutes until the liquid is completely absorbed.

Meanwhile cook the spaghetti in a large pan of salted water until *al dente*.

Drain.

Mix the spaghetti with the beans and serve with grated cheese.

Serves 4
Preparation time: 50–60 minutes
Calories per portion: 945
Recommended wine: Category 4 • 1 • 2

130

Bucatini with Italian salami

2 onions, quartered and sliced

2 cloves garlic, finely diced

⅓ cup olive oil

1¼ cups salami (cacciatore), skinned and diced

½ glass dry white wine

½ teaspoon bouillon granules

fresh rosemary and thyme, or ½ teaspoon each dried rosemary and thyme

freshly grated nutmeg

1 x 14-oz. can tomatoes, drained, deseeded and pulped

salt

freshly ground pepper

14 oz. bucatini

salted water

1 cup coarsely grated caciocavallo cheese

Gently fry the onions and garlic in 5 tablespoons of the olive oil until they are transparent.

Add the salami, white wine, bouillon granules, herbs and nutmeg, and sauté for 5 minutes.

Stir in the tomatoes, cover, cook together for 5–8 minutes, then adjust the seasoning with salt and pepper.

Cook the bucatini in plenty of salted water and 1 tablespoon oil until *al dente*, then drain.

Mix the pasta with the sauce and serve sprinkled with the cheese.

Serves 4
Preparation time: 35 minutes
Calories per portion: 853
Recommended wine: Category 4•3•1

133

Wholewheat Pasta, Soufflés, and Salads

135

Dictionary of Ingredients

Broths These are extremely important as a basic form of seasoning in Italian cuisine. A stockpot must always be simmering on the stove, especially in the northern parts of Italy, and particularly where risotto is popular, as this dish always requires another dash of broth.

The most important broth in Italy is a vegetable broth. It comes from preparing minestrone, the great mixed-vegetable soup, or it is made separately from all the stalks and other parts of the vegetables that are not suitable for adding to the soup. The broth is boiled up time after time, and water and vegetables can be added *ad infinitum* – sometimes it will taste more strongly of this ingredient, sometimes of that, but it will always be good. It can be used to baste roasting vegetables and meats, and to make gravies and sauces.

Meat broth can be made from beef bones and offcuts of meat, or may be a byproduct of boiled beef. In Italy veal, too, is quite often boiled, not always fried or roasted. If you add a few veal bones to such a broth, you have a wonderful gravy, which can be used for all sorts of meat dishes because it has a neutral flavor and good jelling properties. The same is true of chicken broth: if it is concentrated enough, it will have a pleasant but discreet flavor and will bind well.

The king of all broths is that produced in making *bollito misto* (mixed boiled meats): the goodness of the various types of meat and vegetable mixes, combines and is enhanced. To keep this superb mixture pure, pig's feet and boiled sausage for a *bollito misto* are cooked in separate water.

Distilled liquors These can be used to enhance the flavor of sauces or to flambé food. The spirits most widely used in Italian cooking are Cognac and brandy. Grappa, on the other hand, the marc brandy so popular as an after-dinner drink, is hardly ever used, perhaps because its dryness can give sauces a rough, unpleasant edge. The smooth, mature, woody flavor of brandy and the rounded subtlety of Cognac are particularly well suited to sauces based on white meat.

Calvados, whiskey, gin and vodka are very popular with professional chefs in Italy, but are rarely found in the family kitchen.

Dried pulses These are very important in Italian cooking. There are many bean varieties, with a different sort typical in practically every region of Italy. Because they are used extensively, cooks there generally buy dried products from the most recent harvest, which need a relatively short soaking and cooking time, still have their full quotient of valuable protein, and taste much better into the bargain. Lentils and peas in a variety of colors, sizes and flavors also provide extremely valuable nutrients. Be sure to use all dried pulses by the date recommended on the package, and to boil dried kidney beans for at least 10 minutes.

Eggs The quality of eggs can vary. When buying eggs for making pasta or to serve with it, choose the best. If possible, buy eggs from free-range hens fed exclusively on corn.

Flour Generally, pasta is made from durum wheat semolina, or at least durum wheat flour. If the dough is kneaded by hand, all-purpose white flour will be easier to handle. However, especially if you have a pasta machine, you can knead dough and shape pasta from a variety of types of flour, as can be seen in the different regions in Italy.

Flours can be based not only on durum wheat but also on rye, mixed cereals, buckwheat, dried sweet chestnuts or corn.

Honey Strained honey from a beekeeper is to be preferred to commercial products, but there are many good quality honeys on the market. There also are many types of honey derived from different flowers, such as orange or lemon blossom honey, sweet chestnut, and acacia honey.

Nuts and seeds Virtually no other country uses nuts in cooking to the same extent as Italy! There are nut-trees throughout the country, with some areas specializing in the growing of nuts.

The most popular is the walnut. Walnut kernels are essential for baking and sweetmeats, and ground or pounded they can also be used to bind sauces. Often they are just chopped and sprinkled over the dish when it is ready: the uncooked flavor is retained, and the special consistency somewhere between hard and soft is an added attraction.

Pine nuts, almonds, and filberts are almost as highly prized. There is no substitute for the resinous aroma of pine nuts in *pesto genovese,* for example, the basil-based sauce from Genoa.

Melon, pumpkin and sunflower seeds, usually roasted in their own oil, are used to season or garnish dishes after they have been cooked.

When choosing nuts and seeds, it is a mistake to buy cheap ones. Good products, careful tending, and the outlay for harvesting and storage have their price.

Sea salt It is regarded as nutritious and more valuable than ordinary table salt, but table salt was once sea salt too! There is no difference in taste between refined sea salt and table salt; unrefined, grayish sea salt, however, does taste "wilder", like a fresh sea breeze.

Soy sauce Derived from wheat, soy beans and salt, this is one of the oldest and most natural seasonings in the world, originating in China and Japan. It can also improve traditional American and European recipes.

Vinegar In Italy distilled vinegar is used for preserving and wine vinegar is used in cooking. Often distinctions in wine vinegar are based on the place of origin of the wine – there are everyday products and very exclusive varieties from small vineyards. Italian vinegar has a powerful flavor, normally containing 6-8 percent acidity (as against the more usual 5 percent), so when you want it for flavoring you must be more sparing and cautious in its use.

There are also various flavored vinegars available, such as tarragon vinegar and raspberry vinegar. One speciality is balsamic vinegar, lavishly produced from concentrated grape juice and matured through prolonged storage in small casks made of a variety of woods. It was originally a speciality of the Modena district, but is now also produced elsewhere. Balsamic vinegar has an incredible aroma and can turn an otherwise ordinary sauce into a true experience. On the other hand, good quality is expensive. Even if you do not buy the most expensive, you should avoid very cheap products, as they will not have the round aroma and flavor you are looking for.

Wine This is the most important form of liquid seasoning for the sauce chef, indispensable for stews and casseroles. However, there is no such thing as "cooking wine" – wine not fit to drink but good enough to cook with. If you use stale or corked wine in your cooking, you should not be surprised if your sauces leave something to be desired. There is never anything wrong with using some of the wine you will be drinking with the meal in the sauce.

There are a few simple rules to observe:

• White wine, in light sauces, should be dry, light and sparkling, but not too acidic. All Italian white table wines meet these criteria.

• White wine for use in dark sauces should be powerful, full-fruited and possibly even slightly sweet (*vin santo*).

• Red wine should be fruity and powerful, but should not contain too much tannin. Most Italian red wines meet these requirements, though there could be a few problems with some very light, insubstantial wines from northern Italy (South Tyrol, Bardolino, Valpolicella) and some very heavy ones (Nebbiolo, Cabernet). The exception proves the rule: rich sauces made from dark meats and game can take even a Barolo from Piedmont or a Cabernet from Friuli.

• White vermouth, as dry as possible, is often used for light sauces, especially with fish and poultry. The same is true of sherry (fino or manzanilla, or possibly dry amontillado for a very powerful sauce), and, above all, Marsala. We are not talking about the heavy, sweet Marsala, often mixed with egg or aromatic ingredients, but the classic Marsala, which is white and dry (*bianco secco*). The best bottles are labeled *superiore* or *vergine*.

Wholewheat spaghetti with kidney beans

¾ cup dried kidney beans or 2 x 15-oz. cans of kidney beans

1 onion, peeled and quartered

1 bay leaf

1 level teaspoon salt

1 onion, peeled and diced

2 carrots, scrubbed and diced

2 leeks, washed and sliced

4 tablespoons sunflower oil

1 chili pepper, chopped, or a few drops tabasco sauce

½ teaspoon dried sage

½ teaspoon dried thyme

1 tablespoon green peppercorns, preserved

½ teaspoon bouillon granules

½ cup tomato juice

1 tablespoon tomato paste

1 lb. spaghetti

salted water

1 bunch chives, chopped

If using dried beans, soak them overnight in cold water.

Drain and cook the dried beans covered in fresh water with the onion, bay leaf and salt for about 1½ hours, being sure to boil them for at least 10 minutes.

Sauté the second onion, carrots and leeks in oil.

Add the drained beans or the rinsed canned beans, seasonings, tomato juice and tomato paste, and cook for about 20 minutes.

Cook the spaghetti in plenty of salted water until *al dente*.

Drain.

Combine the pasta with the bean mixture and serve sprinkled with the chopped chives.

Serves 4
Preparation time (excluding soaking time): about 2 hours
Calories per portion: 767
Recommended wine: Category 1•3•4

Buckwheat noodles with savoy cabbage and sage

2 cups finely milled buckwheat flour

1 cup all-purpose flour

3 eggs

2 teaspoons salt

1–2 tablespoons water

1⅓ cups peeled and diced potatoes

½ small savoy cabbage, washed and sliced (about 3 cups)

4 quarts vegetable broth

6–8 sage leaves, chopped

1 onion, diced

2 cloves garlic, sliced

2 tablespoons butter

2 tablespoons oil

1 cup grated Parmesan cheese

freshly ground pepper

Mix the two flours and work into a firm dough with the eggs, 1 teaspoon of salt and water; cover and leave to rest.

Roll the pasta dough out thinly and turn through the spaghetti cutters of a pasta machine.

Cook the potatoes and cabbage in the broth with the remaining salt over a low heat for 15–20 minutes, then add the pasta and boil for about 2 minutes on a fierce heat until *al dente*.

Drain.

Meanwhile fry the sage, onion and garlic in the butter and oil until they are golden.

Put alternate layers of the noodle mixture and the cheese into a bowl.

Pour the sage butter over the dish, sprinkle it with pepper and serve.

Serves 4
Preparation time: 70 minutes
  (excluding time pasta has to rest)
Calories per portion: 685
Recommended wine: Category **1**•3•2

Wholewheat spaghetti with walnut sauce

1 cup shelled walnuts
⅓ cup cashew nuts
1 tablespoon pine nuts
⅞ cup light cream
2 tablespoons vegetable broth
1 tablespoon honey
a pinch of salt
2 arugula leaves, finely chopped
14 oz. wholewheat spaghetti
salted water

Divide the walnuts into five equal amounts.

Pour boiling water over two-fifths of the walnuts, leave for 2 minutes, drain and peel.

Roast another two-fifths of the walnuts with the oven set at 195°F for 5 minutes.

Purée the peeled and roasted walnuts, the cashews and pine nuts and cream in a blender or food processor, season with the vegetable broth, honey and salt, and stir in the arugula leaves and the remaining walnuts, chopped.

Cook the spaghetti in plenty of salted water until *al dente*, then drain.

Divide the spaghetti onto 4 plates, pour the sauce over it and serve immediately.

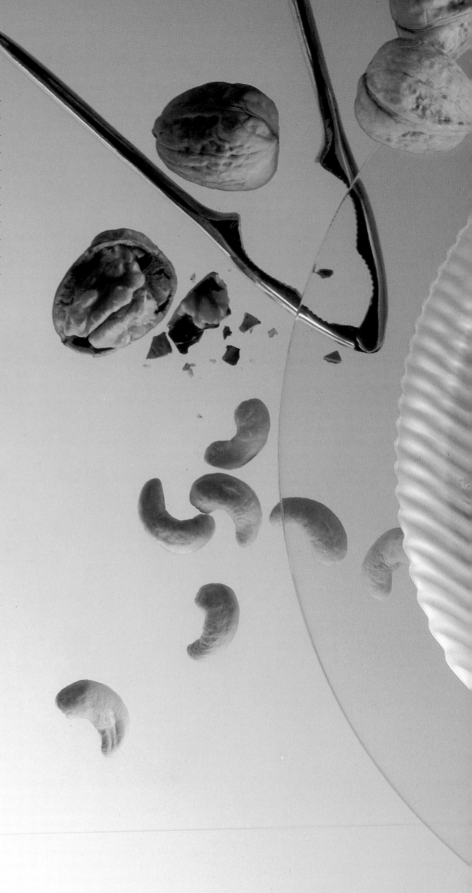

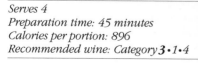

Serves 4
Preparation time: 45 minutes
Calories per portion: 896
Recommended wine: Category 3·1·4

Wholewheat spaghetti with red peppers

3 tablespoons olive oil

1 onion, peeled and cut into strips

2 cloves garlic, finely chopped

3 red peppers, deseeded and finely diced

1 10-oz. package frozen whole kernel corn

½ cup vegetable broth

salt

freshly ground pepper

1 fresh chili pepper, deseeded and chopped, or 1 dried chili pepper, crushed

1 lb. wholewheat spinach spaghetti

salted water

1 tablespoon chopped parsley

Heat the oil in a skillet, and gently fry the onions, garlic and red peppers, stirring from time to time.

Add the corn and vegetable broth, season with salt and pepper and the chili pepper, and cook gently for 10 minutes on a low heat.

Meanwhile cook the spaghetti in plenty of salted water until *al dente*.

Drain.

Mix the spaghetti and the sauce in a bowl, and serve sprinkled with parsley.

Serves 4
Preparation time: 30 minutes
Calories per portion: 677
Recommended wine: Category 4•3•1

Wholewheat tomato spaghetti with onion and buckwheat sauce

2 cups rye flour

2 cups wholewheat flour

⅓ cup concentrated tomato paste

3 eggs

3 tablespoons water

1 teaspoon salt

2 tablespoons cooking oil

⅓ cup olive oil

4 tablespoons butter

2–3 Spanish onions or 1¼ lb. ordinary onions, peeled and finely chopped

2 cloves garlic, finely chopped

½ teaspoon each dried thyme and oregano, or 1 tablespoon each fresh thyme and oregano leaves

⅓ cup buckwheat grain

salt

freshly ground pepper

a pinch of paprika

½ cup water

½ cup sunflower seeds

salted water

Make a pasta dough from the flours, tomato paste, eggs, water, salt and 1 tablespoon cooking oil; cover, and leave to rest for 30 minutes.

Heat the olive oil and butter in a skillet, sauté the onions and garlic until they are transparent, then add the herbs, buckwheat, seasoning, and water, and simmer for 30 minutes.

Lightly brown the sunflower seeds in the remaining cooking oil, then drain.

Roll out the pasta dough, turn it through the spaghetti cutters of a pasta machine, then cook in plenty of salted water until *al dente*, and drain.

Serve the pasta mixed with the buckwheat and onion sauce and the sunflower seeds.

Serves 4
Preparation time: 60 minutes
Calories per portion: 1017
Recommended wine: Category 1•3•2

Bucatini soufflé with broccoli and tomatoes

4 tablespoons olive oil

2 cloves garlic, finely chopped

1½ lb. broccoli, buds separated from stalks, and stalks sliced

1 cup meat broth

salt

freshly ground pepper

3 large beefsteak tomatoes, skinned, cut into 8 pieces, and deseeded

14 oz. bucatini

salted water

2 eggs

⅞ cup milk

1¼ cups taleggio cheese, diced

salt

freshly ground pepper

a pinch of nutmeg

a pinch of paprika

1 tablespoon chopped parsley

½ cup freshly grated Parmesan cheese

1 tablespoon butter

Heat the oil in a skillet, add the garlic and broccoli, and fry gently, turning from time to time.

Pour the broth over the mixture, season with salt and pepper, and cook for 10–15 minutes until tender.

Meanwhile bring the bucatini to the boil in plenty of salted water.

Drain.

Put alternating layers of vegetables and pasta in a buttered soufflé dish.

Beat the eggs together with the milk, broccoli cooking water, diced taleggio, herbs and seasonings, and pour this mixture over the pasta. Top with Parmesan cheese and dots of butter.

Cook in the oven at 400°F for about 35 minutes.

Serves 4
Preparation time: 60 minutes
Calories per portion: 1029
Recommended wine: Category 3·2·1

Capellini and zucchini omelet

2 tablespoons oil

1 onion, chopped

2 cloves garlic, chopped

¼ cup diced bacon, soaked and drained

2 zucchini, diced

½ teaspoon dried thyme

½ teaspoon dried oregano

12 oz. cooked capellini (about 4½ oz. uncooked)

salt

freshly ground pepper

4 eggs

½ cup milk

Put the oil in a large skillet and fry the onion, garlic and bacon over a low heat until golden.

Add the zucchini, thyme and oregano, and continue frying gently.

Mix in the cooked pasta, season with salt and pepper, and stir regularly.

Whisk the eggs with the milk, pour over the pasta and vegetables, cover and cook over a moderate heat until set.

Serve sprinkled with fresh pepper.

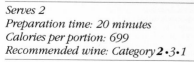

Serves 2
Preparation time: 20 minutes
Calories per portion: 699
Recommended wine: Category 2·3·1

Exotic spaghetti salad

3 chicken breasts

3½ cups instant chicken broth

4 cups chopped celery

1 cup fresh pineapple, diced

12 oz. spaghetti, cooked (about 6 cups)

1 heaping tablespoon mayonnaise

¾ cup plain yogurt

juice of 1 lemon

1 teaspoon curry powder

a pinch of ground red pepper

salt

freshly ground pepper

celery leaves or parsley

Cook the chicken breasts in the broth for 20 minutes until tender.

Remove, skin, take the meat off the bones, and slice.

Mix the spaghetti with the meat, celery and pineapple.

Combine the mayonnaise, yogurt, lemon juice, curry powder, ground red pepper, and season well with salt and pepper.

Fold the sauce into the pasta, then cover and leave to stand for at least 30 minutes to allow the flavors to blend.

Serve with a garnish of celery leaves or parsley.

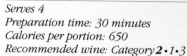

Serves 4
Preparation time: 30 minutes
Calories per portion: 650
Recommended wine: Category 2•1•3

152

153

Provençal pasta pie

8 oz. spaghetti, cooked (4 cups)

4 small uncooked pork sausages

2 eggplants, washed and sliced
   lengthwise

2½ cups sliced button mushrooms,
   cleaned and sliced

2 onions, peeled and cut into rings

⅓ cup olive oil

1 teaspoon dried mixed herbs

salt

freshly ground pepper

2 cups skinned and sliced beefsteak
   tomatoes

4 eggs

½ cup whipping cream

½ cup milk

2 cloves garlic, crushed

¾ cup freshly grated cheese (Gruyère,
   Swiss cheese, Dutch Edam)

1 tablespoon chopped parsley

Cut the cooked spaghetti into
smallish pieces.

Remove the skin from the sausages,
form the sausage meat into balls, and
fry these lightly in a non-stick skillet
to seal.

Sauté the eggplants, mushrooms, and
onions in 4 tablespoons of oil and
season with the mixed herbs, salt
and pepper.

Grease an ovenproof pie plate with 1
tablespoon of oil. Put the spaghetti
and sausage rissoles in it, then
arrange the sautéd vegetables and
the tomatoes decoratively on top.

Beat the remaining ingredients
together, season with salt and
pepper and pour this mixture over
the pasta and vegetables.

Bake in the oven at 350–400°F for
40–45 minutes until set.

Serves 4
Preparation time excluding baking
   time: 30 minutes
Calories per portion: 816
Recommended wine: Category 3•2•4

More Recipes ...
with Vegetables

Bucatini casserole au gratin

1 lb. bucatini

salted water

3 onions, diced

3 cloves garlic, chopped

¼ cup olive or corn oil

1 lb. peppers, washed and cut into strips

1 lb. button mushrooms, cleaned and sliced (10 cups)

2 x 16-oz. cans tomatoes, halved and deseeded, with their juice

1 tablespoon tomato paste

½ teaspoon each of marjoram and thyme

salt

freshly ground pepper

2 tablespoons black olives, pitted and chopped

1 tablespoon chopped parsley

¼ cup freshly grated Parmesan cheese

2 tablespoons breadcrumbs

1½ tablespoons butter

Cook the bucatini in plenty of salted water until *al dente*, then turn into a strainer, refresh with cold water and drain.

Fry the onions and garlic in oil until they are golden.

Add the chili peppers and mushrooms, cook gently, turning from time to time.

Add the tomatoes, tomato juice, tomato paste, herbs and seasoning, and cook for 15 minutes.

Stir in the olives and parsley.

Grease an ovenproof dish, put in a layer of pasta, a layer of vegetables and cover with some cheese. Repeat these layers, sprinkle the remaining cheese and breadcrumbs on top, and dot with butter.

Cook in the oven at 400°F for 35–40 minutes.

Serves 4
Preparation time: 75 minutes
Calories per portion: 851

Baked bucatini

14 oz. bucatini

salted water

1 tablespoon oil

1 medium eggplant, about 1 lb.

salt

1½ tablespoons butter

2 tablespoons sunflower oil

2 cloves garlic, crushed

2 onions, diced

5 cups sliced button mushrooms

1 x 16-oz. can peeled tomatoes, halved and deseeded

1 cup tomato juice

⅞ cup crème fraîche

freshly ground pepper

1 level teaspoon Italian mixed herbs

½ teaspoon thyme

1½ cups grated cheese

1⅓ cups diced cooked ham

small bunch parsley, chopped

2 teaspoons butter

Cook the bucatini in plenty of salted water until *al dente*, then drain, and mix with 1 tablespoon oil.

Meanwhile, cut the eggplant into ¾-in. cubes, sprinkle with salt, and leave standing for 15 minutes, then dry them.

Heat the butter and oil in a skillet, fry the garlic, onions and eggplants until they begin to brown, add the mushrooms, cook gently, then stir in the tomatoes, tomato juice and crème fraîche, and season with salt, pepper and the herbs.

Cook for about 20 minutes over a low heat until tender, then mix in the ham and parsley.

Grease an ovenproof casserole with butter, put in a layer of bucatini, a layer of sauce and some cheese, repeat layers until full, using about 1 cup of the grated cheese; sprinkle the remaining cheese on top.

Bake in the oven at 450–475°F for about 15–20 minutes.

Serves 4
Preparation time: 70 minutes
Calories per portion: 996

Bucatini with onion sauce

⅓ cup olive oil

3 tablespoons butter

2–3 Spanish onions or 8 smaller onions, peeled and thinly sliced

2 cloves garlic, finely chopped

½ teaspoon each dried thyme and oregano (1 tablespoon each if fresh herbs are used)

salt

freshly ground pepper

a pinch of paprika

⅓ cup water

1 lb. bucatini

salted water

1 bunch flat-leaf parsley, chopped

Heat the olive oil and butter in a skillet and fry the onions and garlic gently until they are transparent.

Add the herbs, seasoning and water, and cook until golden.

Cook the bucatini in plenty of salted water until *al dente*.

Drain.

Serve the pasta well mixed with the onion sauce and parsley.

Serves 4
Preparation time: 40 minutes
Calories per portion: 656

Spaghetti with eggplants

3 small eggplants (about 1½ lb.)

1 heaping teaspoon salt

3 cloves garlic, sliced

1 chili pepper, cut into rings

½ cup olive oil

14 oz. spaghetti

salted water

2 tablespoons chopped parsley

freshly ground pepper

Cut the eggplants into slices about ½-in. thick, sprinkle with salt, weight down and leave to draw for about 1 hour.

Brown the garlic and chili pepper in the olive oil, then remove them from the pan.

Dry the slices of eggplant and fry them on both sides in the oil, cooking them in two batches if necessary.

Cook the spaghetti in plenty of salted water until *al dente*.

Drain and put in a bowl.

Arrange the eggplant slices on top, and serve sprinkled with parsley and pepper.

Variation

Toss the spaghetti in tomato sauce.

Spaghetti with broccoli and tomatoes

¼ cup olive oil

2 cloves garlic, finely chopped

1 onion, peeled and diced

1½ lb. broccoli, buds separated from stalks, and stalks sliced

1 cup beef broth

salt

freshly ground pepper

3 large beefsteak tomatoes, skinned, deseeded and diced

1 bunch parsley, chopped

14 oz. spaghetti

salted water

1 cup freshly grated Parmesan cheese

Heat the oil in a skillet, and fry the garlic and onion in it until they are transparent.

Add the broccoli and cook gently, turning from time to time.

Pour in the broth, season with salt and pepper, and cook for about 15 minutes.

Add the diced tomato and the parsley, cover and heat through for just a few minutes.

Meanwhile cook the spaghetti in plenty of salted water until *al dente*.

Drain.

Mix the vegetables with the spaghetti and serve with the Parmesan cheese.

Spaghetti parcels

⅓ cup olive oil

2 cloves garlic, sliced

1 x 16-oz. can peeled tomatoes, drained, halved, deseeded and finely chopped

1 dried chili pepper, crushed

1 level teaspoon salt

freshly ground pepper

14 oz. spaghetti

salted water

8 small ripe tomatoes, skinned, quartered and deseeded

small bunch flat-leaf parsley, finely chopped

2 tablespoons capers

½ cup black olives, pitted

waxed paper

1 bunch basil, coarsely chopped

Heat 4 tablespoons of oil in a skillet, brown the garlic in it, then remove.

Put the diced canned tomatoes, chili pepper, salt and pepper in the pan, and cook for about 20 minutes until the sauce begins to thicken.

Meanwhile cook the spaghetti in plenty of salted water for 8–10 minutes.

Drain.

Mix the spaghetti with the tomato sauce, fresh tomato pieces, parsley, capers and olives. Cut 4 large squares of waxed paper, and distribute the spaghetti mixture between them, sprinkle some olive oil and some freshly ground pepper over each portion.

Make a neat parcel out of each sheet of waxed paper, and put them on a baking sheet. Bake in the oven at 400°F for 15–20 minutes.

Remove the parcels from the oven, put each on a heated plate, cut open and serve sprinkled with basil.

Serves 4
Preparation time: 25 minutes
Calories per portion: 661

Serves 4
Preparation time: 40 minutes
Calories per portion: 831

Serves 4
Preparation time (not including baking time): 45 minutes
Calories per portion: 695

Spaghetti with sage and butter

1 lb. spaghetti

salted water

½ cup butter

10 fresh sage leaves, finely shredded or cut into strips

½ cup beef broth

freshly ground pepper

salt

1 cup freshly grated Parmesan cheese

Cook the spaghetti in plenty of salted water until *al dente*.

Meanwhile melt the butter in a skillet, gently fry the sage, add the broth and continue cooking until somewhat reduced.

Season with salt and pepper, and mix in half of the Parmesan cheese.

Drain the spaghetti.

Combine the pasta with the sage and cheese mixture, and serve with the rest of the cheese.

Highly spiced spaghetti

⅓ cup olive or sunflower oil

1½ tablespoons butter

4 cloves garlic, finely chopped

2 lb. broccoli, buds separated from stalks, and the stalks sliced

2 zucchini, washed and diced

1 teaspoon dried thyme

freshly grated nutmeg

2 fresh chili peppers, deseeded and cut into rings

salt

8 oz. spinach spaghetti

8 oz. ordinary spaghetti

salted water

salt

freshly ground pepper

½ cup freshly grated pecorino cheese

Heat the oil and butter in a deep skillet, and fry the garlic lightly until golden.

Add the broccoli and zucchini without drying them, season with the thyme, nutmeg, chili peppers and salt, cover and cook on a low heat until tender, but still crisp.

Cook the spaghetti in plenty of salted water until *al dente*.

Drain.

Mix the spaghetti with the vegetables, adjust the seasoning with additional salt and pepper if desired.

Serve with the pecorino cheese.

Spaghetti with cold tomato sauce

5 large, ripe beefsteak tomatoes

4 cloves garlic, peeled and finely chopped

1 small chili pepper, deseeded and finely chopped

1 onion, peeled and finely chopped

1 tablespoon black olives, pitted and diced

1 bunch basil, leaves finely shredded

½ to ⅝ cup olive oil

juice of 1 lemon

salt

freshly ground pepper

1 lb. spaghetti or fidelini

salted water

Scald the tomatoes with boiling water, skin, quarter and remove the seeds, and use a fork to mash the flesh.

Mix in the garlic, onion, olives, chili pepper and basil leaves one after the other.

Beat the olive oil into the mixture with the fork, a tablespoonful at a time.

Finally, adjust the flavor with lemon juice, salt and plenty of pepper.

Leave the sauce somewhere cool (not in a refrigerator) for an hour to blend.

Cook the spaghetti in plenty of salted water until *al dente*.

Drain, and serve immediately with the sauce.

Serves 4
Preparation time: 25 minutes
Calories per portion: 789

Serves 4
Preparation time: 45 minutes
Calories per portion: 769

Serves 4
Preparation time: 35 minutes
Calories per portion: 760

Spaghetti with zucchini and button mushrooms

1/3 cup olive oil

2 cloves garlic, peeled and sliced

4 medium zucchini, washed and sliced

salt

freshly ground pepper

1/2 teaspoon each dried thyme and oregano, or fresh herbs

5 cups sliced button mushrooms

1 1/2 tablespoons butter

1 clove garlic, crushed

salt

freshly ground pepper

1/2 teaspoon curry powder

1 cup light cream

1 lb. spaghetti

salted water

Heat 1/4 cup olive oil in a skillet, brown the sliced garlic in it, then remove.

Fry the zucchini in the oil, season with salt, pepper, thyme and oregano, then remove them, too.

Sauté the mushrooms in the remaining oil and the butter, return the zucchini, add the crushed garlic, salt, pepper, curry powder and cream, cover and cook gently for about 15 minutes.

Meanwhile cook the spaghetti in plenty of salted water until *al dente*.

Drain.

Arrange the spaghetti with the vegetables and serve.

Serves 4
Preparation time: 40 minutes
Calories per portion: 838

Spaghettini with black truffle

2 pickled anchovies, well soaked in water, boned and chopped

1/3 cup olive oil

1 bunch parsley, finely chopped

1 black truffle, about the size of an egg, or 2-3 smaller ones equivalent in size, cleaned with a brush, and pared into slivers

14 oz. spaghettini

salted water

Put the anchovies in a small bowl, add the oil drop by drop, mashing the anchovies with a fork.

Stir into a paste, mixing in the parsley and half of the thin slices of truffle.

Cook the spaghettini in plenty of salted water until *al dente*.

Drain.

Turn into a bowl and mix with the paste.

Divide the pasta onto 4 plates and serve with the remaining truffle strewn on top. (Do not serve cheese with this!)

Serves 4
Preparation time: 20 minutes
Calories per portion: 537

...with Cheese

Bucatini with cheese sauce, au gratin

14 oz. bucatini, broken up

salted water

3 tablespoons butter

⅓ cup flour

2¼ cups milk

½ cup mozzarella, diced

½ cup blue-veined cheese without any rind, crumbled

salt

freshly ground pepper

freshly grated nutmeg

1¼ cups grated hard cheese (Gouda, Swiss cheese, Gruyère)

Cook the bucatini in plenty of salted water until *al dente*, then drain.

Melt 2 tablespoons of the butter in a saucepan, add the flour to make a roux, cook for 2 minutes stirring constantly without letting it brown.

Add the milk, using a whisk to beat smooth, keep stirring until the sauce boils, and allow to boil for 1 minute.

Stir the mozzarella and blue-veined cheese into the sauce until melted.

Season to taste with salt, pepper and nutmeg.

Butter an ovenproof casserole dish.

Put in a layer of bucatini, a layer of sauce and a layer of grated cheese, repeat the layers and finish with a layer of sauce and cheese.

Bake in the oven at 400°F for 30–40 minutes until a golden crust has formed.

Serves 4
Preparation time not including baking time: 25 minutes
Calories per portion: 890

Spaghetti with cheese and pepper

1 lb. spaghetti

salted water

¼ cup olive oil

2 cups freshly grated pecorino cheese

freshly ground pepper

salt

Cook the spaghetti in plenty of salted water until *al dente*.

Drain.

Mix the spaghetti with the olive oil, fold in 1½ cups of the pecorino cheese, and sprinkle with pepper.

Adjust the seasoning sparingly with salt.

Serve with the remaining cheese sprinkled on top.

Serves 4
Preparation time: 20 minutes
Calories per portion: 795

Spaghettini with Roquefort sauce

14 oz. spaghettini

salted water

8 oz. Roquefort cheese

¾ cup light cream

1 cup milk

1 small glass Cognac

½–¾ cup pistachio nuts, finely chopped

salt

freshly ground pepper

Cook the spaghettini in plenty of salted water until *al dente*.

Drain.

Cook the Roquefort, cream and milk over a low heat until the cheese melts, then add the Cognac and pistachio nuts.

Season to taste with salt and pepper.

Mix the spaghettini with the cheese sauce and serve immediately.

Serves 4
Preparation time: 20 minutes
Calories per portion: 752

... with Fish and Shellfish

Spaghetti with eel stew

¼ cup olive oil

1 clove garlic, finely chopped

1 onion, diced

2 tablespoons. fresh chopped ginger

1⅓ cup blanched diced celery

1 carrot, diced

1¼ lb. eel, skinned, cleaned and cut into pieces 1 in. thick

1½ lb. ripe tomatoes, skinned, quartered and deseeded

1 cup light, dry red wine

salt

freshly ground pepper

14 oz. spaghetti

salted water

small bunch flat-leaf parsley, chopped

Heat the oil in a deep skillet.

Brown the garlic, onion, ginger, celery and carrot in the oil, add the pieces of eel and sauté, turning from time to time.

Add the quartered tomatoes and the red wine, and simmer for 15–20 minutes over a low heat.

Season with salt and pepper.

Cook the spaghetti in plenty of salted water until *al dente*.

Drain.

Divide the spaghetti onto 4 plates, ladle some eel stew on each, and serve sprinkled with parsley.

Serves 4
Preparation time: 50 minutes
Calories per portion: 954

Spaghetti with seafood

3 cloves garlic, crushed

1 bunch scallions, washed and diced

1½ lb. ripe tomatoes, skinned, deseeded and chopped

2 tablespoons butter

½ cup light cream

1 bay leaf

1 lb. frozen or 1 x 7½-oz. can clams

2⅔ pints fresh mussels, scrubbed and cleaned, or 1 x 7½-oz. can mussels

7 oz. scallops removed from their shells

7 oz. filleted perch, diced

½ cup peeled shrimp

1 tablespoon lemon juice

1 tablespoon chopped herbs (tarragon, chervil, parsley)

salt

freshly ground pepper

1 lb. spaghetti

salted water

Sauté the garlic, scallions and tomatoes in the butter, add the cream and bay leaf, and cook together for 10 minutes.

Add all the seafood and fish, cover and leave to combine (if frozen clams are used, cook them for 5–10 minutes).

Adjust the seasoning with lemon juice, herbs, salt and pepper.

Meanwhile cook the spaghetti in plenty of salted water until *al dente*.

Drain.

Serve at once with the seafood.

Serves 4
Preparation time: 50 minutes
Calories per portion: 810

Spaghetti salad with vinaigrette sauce

14 oz. spaghetti

salted water

4 beefsteak tomatoes, skinned, deseeded and diced

1 x 10-oz. can mussels (flesh only)

½ cup olives, pitted and quartered

2 canned artichoke hearts, quartered

2½ cups mozzarella cheese, diced

¼ cup balsamic vinegar

1 onion, finely chopped

½ cup fresh chopped herbs such as parsley, dillweed, chervil, basil, or tarragon

⅓ cup sunflower oil

½ teaspoon salt

a pinch of sugar

freshly ground pepper

Cook the spaghetti in plenty of salted water until *al dente*.

Turn into a colander, refresh with cold water and drain well.

Place in a bowl and mix with the tomatoes, mussels, olives, artichoke hearts and mozzarella cheese.

Combine the vinegar, onions, herbs, and oil to make the vinaigrette and stir well.

Season with salt, sugar and pepper.

Fold the vinaigrette sauce into the spaghetti salad, leave to stand for about 30 minutes to allow the flavors to blend, then serve.

Spaghetti with anchovies, olives and capers

1 lb. spaghetti

salted water

⅓ cup olive oil

3 cloves garlic, finely chopped

3½ oz. preserved anchovy fillets, soaked in water, patted dry and finely chopped

¾ cup pickled capers, soaked in water for 1 hour (capers preserved in vinegar may be substituted)

⅓ cup black olives, pitted

1 bunch parsley, finely chopped

small bunch fresh oregano, leaves stripped from the stems

salt

freshly ground pepper

Cook the spaghetti in plenty of salted water until *al dente*.

Drain.

While the pasta is cooking, heat the olive oil in a skillet and fry the garlic until it is almost transparent.

Stir in the anchovies, capers and olives.

Combine with the hot pasta, add parsley and oregano, and adjust the seasoning with salt if required.

Serve with a sprinkling of pepper.

Spaghetti with squid

¼ cup olive oil

2 cloves garlic, finely chopped

1 bunch scallions, washed and finely diced

1 carrot, peeled and coarsely grated

1 zucchini, coarsely grated

1 lb. squid, cleaned and prepared, cut into rings

½ teaspoon thyme

1 bunch parsley, chopped

1 bay leaf

1 x 2½-oz. can tomato paste

½ cup dry white wine

1 cup instant bouillon

salt

freshly ground pepper

a pinch of chili powder

1 lb. spaghetti or spaghettini

salted water

1 tablespoon lemon juice

a pinch of sugar

Heat the olive oil in a skillet, and sauté the garlic, onion, carrot, and zucchini.

Add the rings of squid, thyme and half of the parsley, and stew for about 5 minutes stirring constantly.

Stir in the bay leaf, tomato paste, wine and bouillon, season with salt, pepper and chili powder, and cook together for about 20 minutes on a low heat.

Cook the spaghetti or spaghettini in plenty of salted water until *al dente*.

Drain and divide onto 4 plates.

Adjust the flavor of the sauce with lemon juice and a pinch of sugar, pour over the pasta and serve sprinkled with the rest of the parsley.

Serves 4
Preparation time (excluding standing time): 30 minutes
Calories per portion: 873

Serves 4
Preparation time: 25 minutes
Calories per portion: 770

Serves 4
Preparation time: 40 minutes
Calories per portion: 745

... *with Meat*

Bucatini with tomato and bacon sauce

1¼ cups slab bacon, roughly diced

2 tablespoons olive oil

1 onion, peeled and finely chopped

1¾ lb. beefsteak tomatoes, skinned, halved, deseeded and thinly sliced

1 fresh chili pepper, chopped, or 1 dried chili pepper, crushed

salt

freshly ground pepper

14 oz. bucatini

salted water

1 cup freshly grated pecorino cheese

Fry the bacon in hot olive oil until crisp, then remove and keep hot.

Sauté the onion in the remaining fat until it is golden.

Add the tomatoes and chili pepper, cook for about 10 minutes, and season to taste with salt and pepper.

Meanwhile cook the bucatini in plenty of salted water until al dente.

Drain.

Place the pasta in a serving bowl and mix with enough of the tomato sauce to give it just a thin covering.

Mix in the bacon and cheese, and serve immediately.

Serves 4
Preparation time: 40 minutes
Calories per portion: 865

Spaghetti tricolore *with prosciutto*

1 lb. red, green and white spaghetti

salted water

3 tablespoons butter

½ cup flaked almonds

5 cups sliced button mushrooms

2 cloves garlic, finely chopped

2 tablespoons capers

20 green olives, pitted

salt

freshly ground pepper

12 thin slices prosciutto

¾ cup freshly grated Parmesan cheese

Cook the spaghetti in plenty of salted water until *al dente*.

Drain.

Melt half of the butter in a skillet; brown the almonds, and remove.

Melt the remaining butter in the same skillet, and sauté the mushrooms and garlic.

Add the capers and olives.

Combine the sauce with the spaghetti, and season with salt and pepper.

Divide the pasta between 4 plates, and put 3 slices of ham on each.

Serve sprinkled with Parmesan cheese and almonds.

Serves 4
Preparation time: 35 minutes
Calories per portion: 850

Spaghetti with chicken curry

2 tablespoons butter

1 tablespoon oil

2 cloves garlic, finely chopped

5 teaspoons finely chopped root ginger

1 onion, finely chopped

1¼ lb. boned chicken breast, cut into narrow strips

1 leek, cut into rings

4 canned pineapple rings, diced

1 teaspoon each hot and mild curry powder

1 cup instant chicken broth

½ cup dry white wine

1 level teaspoon salt

⅓ cup flaked coconut

a pinch of sugar

14 oz. spaghetti

salted water

small bunch flat-leaf parsley, chopped

Heat the butter and oil in a skillet and fry the garlic, ginger and onion until they are transparent.

Add the chicken and leek, and sauté.

Add the pineapple, curry powder, broth and wine, salt and cook for about 20 minutes on a low heat.

Adjust the flavor with the coconut and sugar.

Cook the spaghetti in plenty of salted water until *al dente.*

Drain.

Serve the spaghetti with the chicken curry and sprinkle with parsley.

Spaghetti with bacon and egg

1 lb. spaghetti

salted water

6 slices bacon, finely diced

1½ tablespoons butter

8 eggs

salt

freshly ground pepper

1 bunch chives, chopped

Cook the spaghetti in plenty of salted water until *al dente.*

Drain.

Fry the bacon in the butter, then add the spaghetti.

Beat the eggs well with salt and pepper, pour over the spaghetti, and cook until set, turning occasionally.

Divide onto 4 plates and sprinkle with chopped chives.

Spaghetti with spinach and sweetbreads

1½ lb. calves' sweetbreads

14 oz. tomato spaghetti

salted water

2 scallions, finely chopped

2 cloves garlic, crushed

2 tablespoons butter

¼ cup flour

¼ teaspoon salt

1⅓ cups light cream

1½ lb. young spinach, washed, picked over and scalded with boiling water

salt

ground red pepper

Leave the sweetbreads under gently running water until the water runs clean, then poach for about 6 minutes in boiling water, refresh in cold water, remove any skin, and cut into ¾-in. cubes.

Cook the spaghetti in plenty of salted water until *al dente.*

Drain.

Sauté the onions and garlic in the butter.

Coat the pieces of sweetbreads in salted flour, and braise in the butter.

Add the cream and the spinach, cook for 2 minutes, and season to taste with salt and ground red pepper.

Fold the spaghetti into the sauce and serve at once.

Serves 4
Preparation time: 40 minutes
Calories per portion: 742

Serves 4
Preparation time: 25 minutes
Calories per portion: 907

Serves 4
Preparation time: 40 minutes
Calories per portion: 927

... with wholewheat pasta

Wholewheat pasta soufflé with vegetables

12 oz. wholewheat macaroni

salted water

2 carrots

2 leeks

½ small head of celery

2 tablespoons olive oil

1 cup yeast bouillon

1 cup light cream

nutmeg

sweet paprika

salt

freshly ground pepper

½ cup grated cheese (a mixture of mature Gouda and Swiss cheese)

1 egg

2 tablespoons chopped parsley

Cook the macaroni in plenty of salted water until *al dente*.

Cut the vegetables into julienne strips and sauté briefly in the hot olive oil.

Pour in the yeast bouillon and cook for 10 minutes.

Put alternate layers of macaroni and vegetables in a greased soufflé dish.

Combine the cream with the remaining ingredients, except the parsley, and pour the mixture over the macaroni and vegetables.

Bake in the oven at 400°F for about 20 minutes.

Sprinkle with chopped parsley and serve.

Serves 4
Preparation time: 50 minutes
Calories per portion: 826

Wholewheat spaghetti with button mushrooms and tomatoes

1 bunch scallions, washed and cut into rings

2 cloves garlic, finely chopped

1 lb. fresh button mushrooms, cleaned and sliced (about 8 cups)

2 tablespoons butter or oil

1 level tablespoon flour

1 cup vegetable or chicken broth

½ cup dry white wine

½ teaspoon dried thyme

2 tablespoons crème fraîche

4 large beefsteak tomatoes, skinned, deseeded and diced

salt

freshly ground pepper

1 lb. wholewheat spaghetti

salted water

Sauté the scallions, garlic and mushrooms in butter or oil, sprinkle in the flour, stir in the broth, wine and thyme, and cook for 15 minutes.

Add the crème fraîche and tomatoes, and cook for a further 5 minutes.

Season with salt and pepper.

Meanwhile cook the wholewheat spaghetti in plenty of salted water until *al dente*.

Drain.

Serve the spaghetti mixed with the vegetables.

Serves 4
Preparation time: 40 minutes
Calories per portion: 637

166

Wholewheat spinach spaghetti with mushroom sauce

½ cup dried cèpes

3 onions, diced

8 oz. ham steak, diced (about 1⅓ cups)

1 tablespoon butter

1 lb. brown mushrooms, washed and sliced

½ teaspoon dried marjoram

½ teaspoon dried thyme

½ cup broth

1 cup light cream

salt

freshly ground pepper

1 tablespoon finely chopped flat-leaf parsley

1 lb. wholewheat spinach spaghetti

salted water

½ cup freshly grated Parmesan cheese

Soak the dried cèpes in a cup of hot water for 20 minutes.

Fry the onions and ham steak in a skillet until golden.

Add the butter and the mushrooms, and lightly brown them, turning them from time to time.

Add the dried herbs, the cèpes and the water in which they have soaked, the broth and cream, and cook for 15–20 minutes.

Adjust the seasoning with salt, pepper and parsley.

Cook the spaghetti in plenty of salted water until *al dente*.

Drain.

Divide the spaghetti onto 4 plates, share the sauce between them, and hand around a bowl of Parmesan cheese.

Serves 4
Preparation time: 50 minutes
Calories per portion: 826

Wholewheat spaghetti with vegetables

3 tablespoons olive oil

2 tablespoons butter

1 medium-sized onion, sliced

2 medium-sized zucchini, sliced

1½ cups snow peas, washed and scalded with salted boiling water

3 cups sliced button mushrooms

2 cloves garlic, crushed

1 teaspoon dried thyme

salt

freshly ground pepper

1 lb. wholewheat spaghetti

salted water

¾ cup freshly grated Parmesan cheese

Heat the oil and butter in a large skillet.

Put in the onions, zucchini, snow peas and mushrooms, season with garlic, thyme, salt and pepper, and cook until tender, turning frequently.

Cook the wholewheat spaghetti in plenty of salted water until *al dente*.

Drain.

Mix the spaghetti with the vegetables, divide onto 4 plates, sprinkle cheese on top, and serve.

Serves 4
Preparation time: 35 minutes
Calories per portion: 731

Wine

Wine glasses and wine

Wine, in case you were in any doubt about it, is drunk from a glass. It is true that Roman legionaries drank from a cow horn, Greek shepherds from a goatskin, the medieval guild members favored a pewter goblet and mountain peasants living at one with nature drink from a wooden beaker, but for us it has to be a glass. Only glass is completely free of any taste, resistant to acid, and can be washed so clean that it in no way impairs the balanced aroma of the wine. Even so, wine is affected by the glass from which it is drunk: the shape of the glass can enhance or suppress one component or another in the bouquet, encourage a wine to express itself harmoniously, subtly, strongly or powerfully, or fragment its complexity and destroy its bouquet. It is no accident that different shapes of glass have come to be used in the various wine-growing areas. Of course they were not developed deliberately; wine drinkers just realized that a moselle wine tastes especially good when drunk from one type of glass, while a burgundy tastes best from another.

Since time immemorial glass manufacturers have not hesitated to vary the basic forms according to the fashion of the day, offering designs to suit every trend. There are colored glasses, cut glasses, thin-sided glasses, heavy goblets, simple shapes and elaborate ones. Ultimately, the style of the glass became more important than its purpose; the role played by shape in developing the taste of the wine was forgotten, and many wine glasses were designed to look good with china and to help furnish the dining room. Many people no longer knew which wine could really be enjoyed from which glass – at most they could tell that white wine should be drunk from a small glass and red wine from a large one.

Admittedly, major glass manufacturers and famous designers have always endeavored to harmonize the glass and the wine – with varying results. One person to pursue such considerations to their logical conclusion and design truly pioneering glassware was the Austrian Claus Josef Riedel, whose family had been making glass for nine generations. His aim was to unite in modern glassware designs those elements recognized by people with practical experience and those identified by scientists. In a prolonged, creative dialog with individuals who had an interest in the perfect enjoyment of wine – vintners, connoisseurs, wine-tasters and *sommeliers* (wine-waiters) – as well as physiologists concerned with the receptivity of the tongue, and designers who could give the glasses form, he arrived at the following conclusions:

'For full enjoyment you must use all five senses: that is, you must see, touch, smell, taste and hear. To satisfy the first sense, sight, the receptacle should be undecorated because only then can we see, understand and judge the wine, its color and sparkle.

'To stimulate the second and third senses, touch and smell, to the full, the glass must be thin; thick-sided glasses have a temperature of their own, which is imparted to the wine, so distorting the aroma, the wine's bouquet. The size of the glass is also important: the older and more aromatic the wine, the greater the capacity of the glass should be.

Thus you should have a large glass for a Mouton Rothschild, a medium-sized one of the same shape for a Barolo, a wide-bellied one for a burgundy, and an ovoid one for a young white wine. The upper rim of the glass should never curve like a lily; when you lift the glass from the table to your mouth, the rim of such a shape cuts through the stationary air in the room, and the aroma escaping from the wine as a result of the impact is blown away, so that when you put the glass to your mouth and inhale you no longer detect the smell of the wine – a sign of its quality.

'To allow the fourth sense, taste, to develop fully you should never drink wine from a metal goblet. Induction currents are set up between the wine, which contains dissolved salts, the metal vessel, saliva in the mouth and any fillings in the teeth, introducing a foreign taste. If the correct shape of glass is used, however, the wine can even be enhanced. When designing glasses, the individual wines must be considered so that the tip of the tongue can taste acidity, the whole rim of the tongue perceive sweetness and the end of the tongue recognize any salty or bitter elements. What happens physiologically when we drink from a glass of the shape used for Moselle wines is that we have to suck – sipping is impossible. If you suck, the wine comes onto the end of the tongue and any saltiness and bitterness is filtered out there; it then runs over the edge of the tongue, which registers sweetness, and only a little of the fruit acid reaches the tip of the tongue. This exemplifies how a wine with powerful natural fruit acid can be enjoyed at its best. While this rule applies to wine that tends to be acidic, the rule imposing an ovoid goblet for a sweetish wine is equally correct. You can sip out of an ovoid glass, and if you sip, the tip of the tongue makes contact, the subtle fruit acid is filtered out, the rim of the tongue, which detects sweetness, is touched and the wine reaches the end of the tongue with its salty, bitter qualities intact. Thus this wine, too, achieves its full potential.'

On pages 174-5 you will see which glass has which functions and which wine will exploit them to the full.

The right wine

You can find wine that goes well with both plain and elaborate pasta dishes everywhere. Anyone at all curious and willing to be adventurous in discovering new tastes will enjoy the challenge of trying out a variety of wines to select the right one for each pasta dish. It is easy for Italians – they live with wine, and some simply always drink the wine of the region in which they live. It is harder for us because we have the torment of having to choose from a wider selection, but that can be a charm in itself.

To make things a bit easier for you we have tried to find the most suitable type of wine for each recipe. This leads to the fundamental question of what we are trying to achieve in choosing a wine: harmony between the food and wine – a quiet complementing of tastes – or a contrast, where the taste constituents challenge one another? Everyone has to make this decision personally, so while our recommendations are never wrong, they are not the only possible choices.

You need to allow time for eating and drinking. A wine that may satisfy you after a quick trial may reveal unexpected deficiencies in the course of an extended meal. On the other hand, a simple wine in conjunction with the right food may be surprisingly good. So take your time over getting to know the wines we have recommended, especially the simple ones. In the final analysis a plain spaghetti dish, delicious because it has been perfectly cooked, does not need to be accompanied by a very expensive top-class wine – just a good, really appropriate one to complete your enjoyment.

After making our first selection we checked our suggestions using a test which we can unreservedly recommend to you; it is good fun, forms a lively talking point at the table, reveals a lot, and is quite simply enjoyable. Arrange a meal with pasta and invite a few friends to join you. Choose four recipes from the book, each with a different emphasis, for instance fish, herbs, meat, and cheese. Buy eight wines based on our recommendations. Provide each guest with eight glasses, so that all eight wines can be served with each course. (You may wish to reduce the number of courses to suit your appetite and the number of glasses available!) Mask the wine bottles completely and give each one a number. Give each person a card on which to take notes about which wines go best with each of the different dishes. Many a fond belief regarding wine will be shattered when the bottles are revealed!

On the basis of these experiments we have established a wine typology – you will find the categories on pages 176– 87. Of course, it can, and is intended to, provide only broad outlines. Thus, although the bottles shown represent some of the European wines that are widely available in the homeland of spaghetti, there are also excellent American and Australian wines made from many of the same grape varieties. The wines illustrated are merely examples of the types of wine. Individual wines made from the same grape variety from a clearly defined area with the same basic characteristics can be completely different. The wine also depends on the individual vineyard or slope, its soil and microclimate, the viticulture, the vinification, the vintage and even the vintner. Therefore, because the emphasis here is on type, accompanying every recipe is a picture of a glass indicating whether white, red, rosé, or sparkling wine will suit the dish best. The main recommendation is printed in bold type.

For more information on choosing wine, see page 188.

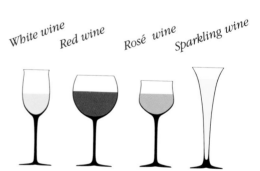

White wine   Red wine   Rosé wine   Sparkling wine

Light white wine

The slender glass with its slightly narrower top retains the delicate, fleeting aromas. The bouquet is not overemphasized, and the relatively small exposed surface allows only restricted evaporation of the aromatic substances. The fruity, flowery fragrances are elegantly accentuated, and the wine's sparkle can be detected in the nose. The outward curve of the rim takes the wine straight on to the tip of the tongue: the carbon dioxide present in young wine is perceived as refreshing, with the fruit acid and sparkle determining the first impression. Then the wine reaches the middle and end of the tongue, and its flavor and roundness can be appreciated. However, the dominant note always comes from the tip of the tongue. The glass is equally well suited to young Rieslings, Silvaners and Müller-Thurgaus, the gentler Chenins Blancs and Sauvignons and all the dry Italian white wines that go so well with pasta.

Powerful white wine

The rather wider but shorter glass shows off more powerful white wines to advantage, the ones that are not so gently fruity, but heavier. This applies to all older white wines where the acidity has subsided to some extent, but particularly to all kinds that have more body right from the start, generally more alcohol and, above all, a certain maturity. The wine can breathe well through the larger surface, the generous aromas can develop, and the bouquet can achieve its proper fullness. This glass is therefore ideal for *Spätlese* and *Auslese* Rieslings and Silvaners, and especially for all the white wines belonging to the burgundy family, irrespective of their country of origin. Pinot Blanc, Chardonnay, Pinot Gris, and the very mature and full rosés taste best drunk from this glass. It is also suitable for all superior, older white wines particularly those from Bordeaux, Spain, Côtes-du-Rhône, and Italy.

Burgundy

Distinguished red wines demand a large, wide, bulging glass so that they can to develop their aroma. A large surface gives the rich fruit a chance to develop and collect above the wine. The wide form emphasizes the fullness of the bouquet, and the wide opening allows sufficient oxygen to reach the wine to enable it to become rounded. Of course, even this glass should be filled only a third full to a half full at most.

This shape is ideal not only for burgundies, but also for Barolo, Barbaresco, Gattinara and the other wines made from the Nebbiolo grape. And, finally, it is suitable for powerful German red wines and Gamay from Beaujolais.

Burgundy goblet

This glass should be used only for the truly great wines from Burgundy and Piedmont, the best vineyards and the great years – lesser ones will be lost in it. Fill the glass just a quarter full, preferably even less – the older the wine, the more space it needs to be able to develop. The very slight outward curve at the rim of the glass carries the precious wine straight to the right taste buds on the tongue so that perception can be developed to the maximum.

174

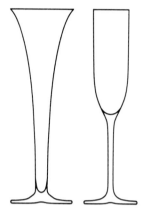

Bordeaux

This glass is slimmer than the one used for burgundy wines, but considerably taller. It concentrates the aroma of expressive wines, makes them less expansive and more elegant. Primarily it counters the tendency to great breadth that can be a feature of heavy Bordeaux wines in particular, and of Californian and Australian red wines, too. It is the glass for the great wines made from the Cabernet Sauvignon and Merlot grapes from any wine-growing area in the world. It also shows off to perfection wines from Tuscany (Chianti, Brunello di Montalcino, Vino Nobile di Montepulciano) and from the Rioja district. The tulip shape is the most universally valid – not only virtually any red wine, but champagne and powerful white wines, too, can be drunk from it if the ideal glass is not available. If you are not sure which type of glass you should use for which red wine, then begin by trying out the wine in this one.

Bordeaux goblet

Use this for the really top wines of the areas just mentioned. Never fill the glass more than a quarter full, so that the wine has room to develop its powerful bouquet. The large surface and the height of the glass are in a harmonious relationship that really flatters the wine, and the aromas and flavors blend and open up to provide an intense experience.

Rosé

This glass combines the attributes of the glasses for burgundy and young white wines. Rosé, which is pressed from red grapes but not fermented with the skins, can develop its "red" fruit and its "white" acidity and freshness to best advantage in it. The width of the glass allows the delicate bouquet to rise above the surface of the wine. When you drink, the lipped rim takes the wine straight onto the tip of the tongue, where it can reveal its carbonated freshness. This is the right glass, too, for light red wines.

Champagne and sparkling wines

In a tall flute glass the sparkling wine can rest, and the rising bubbles are displayed to full advantage. The fruit of the wine is slightly emphasized. The glass is ideal for all branded champagnes and good sparkling wines with a fine *mousse* that are made by the champagne method and matured in the bottle.

For both the most distinguished, subtle and gentle champagnes and the powerful, matured vintage champagnes, a glass that is not quite so tall and has slightly bulging sides is more suitable, emphasizing the balance and the fruit of the bouquet.

German *Sekt* or *vins mousseux* with bigger bubbles and matured in vats should be served in outward curving glasses; the wine makes better contact with the tongue, not leaping over the edge of the glass and fizzing around in the mouth.

Category 1

Light white wines

Dry, perfectly fermented, so no sweetness can be detected. Fairly soft in the mouth – the wine's acidity is perceptible, but not intrusive. The fruit is discreet, never domineering. The overall impression given by these wines is light with a harmonious to neutral taste.

Orvieto

Soave

Frascati

Country of origin:	Italy	Italy	Italy
Wine region:	Umbria	Veneto	Latium
Grape variety:	Malvasia, Trebbiano, Druppegio	Trebbiano, Garganega	Trebbiano, Malvasia
Quality:	D.O.C.	D.O.C.	D.O.C.

Verdicchio

Vernaccia

Provence

Graves

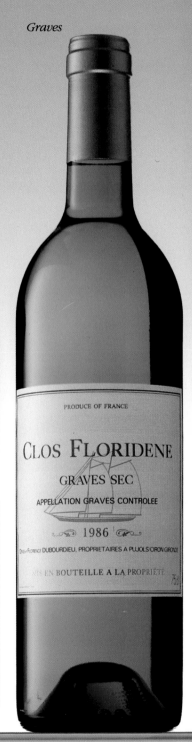

Italy	Italy	France	France
Marches	Tuscany	Aix-en-Provence	Bordeaux-Graves
Verdicchio	Vernaccia	Sauvignon, Uni Blanc	Semillon, Sauvignon, Muscadelle
D.O.C.	D.O.C.	A.C.	A.C.

Category 2

Powerful white wines

Dry, or tasting dry, because the residual sweetness sometimes present is balanced by a clearly discernible acidity. The wines have body, and the alcohol ensures a certain fullness. Depending on the grape variety, this type of wine can be fruity or aromatic to the point of tasting clearly of grapes.

Arneis

Chardonnay

Pinot Grigio

Country of origin:	Italy	Italy	Italy
Wine region:	Piedmont	Veneto	Friuli
Grape variety:	Arneis	Chardonnay	Pinot Grigio
Quality:	V.d.T.	V.d.T.	D.O.C.

Entre-Deux-Mers	Muscadet	Sauvignon	Riesling
France	France	France	France
Bordeaux	Loire	Burgundy	Alsace
Sauvignon	Muscadet	Sauvignon	Riesling
A.C.	A.C.	V.D.Q.S.	A.C.

Riesling

Riesling

Silvaner

Germany	Germany	Germany
Rheingau	Rheinhessen	Rheinhessen
Riesling	Riesling	Silvaner
Q.b.A.	Q.b.A.	Kabinett

Category 3

Rosé and Weissherbst

A light, fresh, neutral taste, but powerful enough to accompany highly seasoned food, which many pasta dishes are. Containing less tannin than red wines, rosés combine agreeableness with a clear fruit and discreet acid, which give them adequate character. They are very adaptable and in many cases prove the ideal accompaniment.

Rosato

Montepulciano

Tavel

Country of origin:	Italy	Italy	France
Wine region:	Latium	Abruzzi	Southern Rhône
Grape variety:	Cesanese, Merlot, Sangiovese	Montepulciano	Grenache, Cinsault, Clairette-Bourb
Quality:	V.d.T.	D.O.C.	A.C.

Pinot Noir

Provence

Category 4

Light red wines

Structured to be dry, but retaining as much fruitiness as possible. Light-colored, aromatic, gentle on the tongue and fresh, these wines should be drunk young. Attractive wines, mild to delicately tart, a lively fruit acid, but not much tannin. The alcohol and body are not very pronounced, lacking the complexity and power of great wines.

France	France	**Country of origin:**
Aix-en-Provence	Alsace	**Wine region:**
Grenache-Cinsault	Pinot Noir	**Grape variety:**
A.C.	A.C.	**Quality:**

	Morellino	Cabernet	Valpolicella	Chianti
Italy	Italy	Italy	Italy	
Tuscany	Piave/Veneto	Veneto	Tuscany	
Sangiovese (Morellino)	Cabernet	Corvina, Molinara, Rondinella	Sangiovese, Canaiolo, Trebbiano	
D.O.C.	D.O.C.-Riserva	D.O.C.	D.O.C.	

183

Marzemino

Merlot

Côtes-du-Rhône

Chenas

Italy	Italy	France	France
Trentino	Friuli	Rhône	Beaujolais
Marzemino	Merlot	Grenache, Cinsault, Carignan	Gamay
D.O.C.	D.O.C.	A.C.	Grand Cru Beaujolais A.C.

Category 5

Powerful red wines

Great body, depth and fruit. They are mostly dark in colour with a pronounced aroma, a high alcohol content and a clearly perceptible tannin, which can be felt on the tongue. As a rule they go better with roasts than with spaghetti, but if spaghetti is served with a rich meat sauce, then a powerful red wine can sometimes be just what is needed.

Spätburgunder

Dolcetto

Barolo

Germany	**Country of origin:**	Italy	Italy
Ahr	**Wine region:**	Piedmont	Piedmont
Spätburgunder	**Grape variety:**	Dolcetto	Nebbiolo
Q.b.A.	**Quality:**	D.O.C.	D.O.C.G.-Riserva

Vino Nobile

Bordeaux

Rioja

Category 6

Sparkling wines

Full sauces flavored with wine can go well with a medium-dry Sekt, or even a dry Spumante (in a shallow "coupe"). To accompany sharp, light sauces, try a *Sekt* made from Riesling grapes or Prosecco Brut (in a flute glass), while a richly creamy light sauce is enhanced by Champagne Brut (in a tulip glass).

Italy	France	Spain	**Country of origin:**
Tuscany	Bordeaux-Médoc	Rioja	**Wine region:**
Canaiolo, Malvasia, Trebbiano	Cabernet Sauvignon, Merlot	Tempranillo, Garnacha	**Grape variety:**
D.O.C.G.-Riserva	A.C.	D.O.	**Quality:**

186

Spumante	Sekt	Champagne

Italy	Germany	France
Piedmont	Rheingau	Champagne
Cortese	Riesling	Chardonnay-Pinot Noir
D.O.C.	Méthode Champenoise	Champagne

Tips for Buying and Serving Wine

The label on the bottle is the wine's visiting card. Anyone who can read the label properly will be spared the worst disappointments. The illustration explains the key words, using an Italian wine as an example. The same basic information will be found on the labels of bottles from most countries; there are just a few minor variations as regards grading and the area where the grapes are grown.

If you want to know more about a wine before you buy than the information supplied on the label, you should seek advice, preferably from a wine merchant who can describe and explain wines to you. Ideally, you should be able to sample the wines, if possible with an expert commentary. Although it is not always so, price is often a guide to a wine's quality: no one can expect to buy top-quality wine for a pittance, and "bargain offers" often prove a disappointment at home. Good vintners and bottlers do not give away their product, but they are not sharks either.

There are, of course, some wines that are less expensive than others. The price/performance gradient is larger than many people think. Wines that are fashionable or in short supply are naturally more expensive than those that are plentiful or not widely known. Diligent wine-lovers who keep their eyes open can make incredible finds. As a rule, follow these simple precepts:

• You are better off with an expensive wine from a less well-known or highly classified area than a cheap wine from a famous area.

• It is better to buy a simple wine from a good firm than a vintage wine from a questionable one.

• Choose a lesser year from a great vineyard rather than a great year from a "potato field".

And finally, there are good grounds for believing that a well-designed, clear label promises a better wine than a florid, cluttered one.

Besides the right glass, the temperature at which wine is served is extremely important for its perfect enjoyment. White wine that is too warm can taste insipid, and red wine that is too cold may have no aroma. For years red wines were served too warm because the normal "room temperature" in most houses had risen by several degrees over the past 100 years. Now they are now being served cooler again: 57–60°F for light red wines and 62–66°F for heavy red wines are regarded as the perfect temperatures.

Light white wines are best enjoyed at 46–50°F, and full white wines and rosés at 52–55°F. This does not mean these wines should be served at these temperatures – they should, in fact, always be served a few degrees cooler, because wine quickly warms up once poured. It depends, of course, on the ambient temperature, if it is really hot, to enjoy white wine properly you should serve it from an ice bucket.

What the Label Tells You

1. ——

2. ——

3. ——

4. ——

5. ——

6. ——

7. ——

8. ——

9. ——

10. ——

1. **Official code number**
   Guarantees that production rules are being observed and that testing has been carried out

2. **Seal of the protective consortia**
   Provides an extra guarantee of quality

3. **Year of vintage**
   An important indication of youth (for white wine or rosé) or age that will improve the quality (especially in the case of powerful red wines)

4. **Source**
   Place of origin

5. **Quality level**
   Appelation Controllé (A.C), *Denominazione di Origine Controllata* (D.O.C) and *Qualitätswein eines bestimmten Anbaugebietes* (Q.b.A) all indicate a quality wine from a specified region. *Garantita* (guaranteed) added to D.O.C. promises outstanding quality in Italian wine, while *Vin Delimité de Qualité Supérieure* (V.D.Q.S.) refers to the second quality of French wines, and *Kabinett* describes a German wine made from simply ripe grapes. *Vino da Tavola, Vin de Table* and *Tafelwein* describe table wine. In addition, the following descriptions may be given to specific wines:
   Classico comes from the heart of the area of origin;
   Riserva has been stored for a longer period;
   Superiore is of higher quality.

6. **Bottled at its place of origin or by the producer**
   The latter is a further guarantee of good quality

7. **Name, company status and address of producer/bottler**

8. **Country of origin**

9. **Net capacity**

10. **Alcohol content**

Index of Recipes